ACT Daily Journal

Get Unstuck & Live Fully With Acceptance & Commitment Therapy

Diana Hill, PhD
Debbie Sorensen, PhD

16pt

Copyright Page from the Original Book

Publisher's Note

This publication is designed to provide accurate and authoritative information in regard to the subject matter covered. It is sold with the understanding that the publisher is not engaged in rendering psychological, financial, legal, or other professional services. If expert assistance or counseling is needed, the services of a competent professional should be sought.

NEW HARBINGER PUBLICATIONS is a registered trademark of
New Harbinger Publications, Inc.

In consideration of evolving American English usage standards, and reflecting a commitment to equity for all genders, "they/them" is used in this book to denote singular persons.

Distributed in Canada by Raincoast Books

Copyright © 2021 by Diana Hill and Debbie Sorensen
               New Harbinger Publications, Inc.
               5674 Shattuck Avenue
               Oakland, CA 94609
               www.newharbinger.com

The meditation that appears in Week 8, Day 5 is from AWAKENING TOGETHER: THE SPIRITUAL PRACTICE OF INCLUSIVITY AND COMMUNITY by Larry Yang, copyright © 2017 Larry Yang. Used by permission of Wisdom Publications.

Cover design by Amy Shoup; Acquired by Elizabeth Hollis Hansen; Edited by James Lainsbury

All Rights Reserved

Library of Congress Cataloging-in-Publication Data

Names: Hill, Diana, (Psychotherapy) author. | Sorensen, Debbie, author.
Title: ACT daily journal : get unstuck and live fully with acceptance and commitment therapy / Diana Hill, PhD, Debbie Sorensen, PhD.
Other titles: Acceptance and commitment therapy daily journal
Description: Oakland : New Harbinger Publications, 2021. | Includes bibliographical references.

Subjects: LCSH: Acceptance and commitment therapy. | Psychotherapy.
Classification: LCC RC489.A32 H55 2021 (print) | LCC RC489.A32 (ebook) | DDC 616.89/1425--dc23
LC record available at https://lccn.loc.gov/2020049513
LC ebook record available at https://lccn.loc.gov/2020049514

Printed in the United States of America

23   22   21
10 9 8 7 6 5 4 3 2 1   First Printing

TABLE OF CONTENTS

Foreword: The Joy, Pain, and Value of Practice	ix
Welcome: Painting the Golden Gate Bridge	xiii
Week 1: Prepare the Ground	1
Week 2: Being Present—Live in the Now	37
Week 3: Cognitive Defusion—Greet the Monsters in Your Head	74
Week 4: Acceptance—Courageous, Willing, and Open	114
Week 5: Perspective Taking—Take In the View	154
Week 6: Values—Choose Your Direction	188
Week 7: Committed Action—Fall on Purpose	227
Week 8: Flexible Integration—Hive Mind	266
The Labyrinth Ahead	303
Additional Resources	308
Acknowledgments	316
References	321
Back Cover Material	339

"Reading this book is like talking with a good friend who happens to be a world-class therapist. It is both simple and profound, practical and soulful, healing and inspiring. It is a rare achievement to find so much wisdom expressed in such a warm and encouraging way. Useful for anxiety and stress, as well as for simply living life fully and joyfully. This is a real gem."
—**Rick Hanson, PhD,** author of *Hardwiring Happiness*

"I love the *ACT Daily Journal!* It is an easy-to-follow guide for practicing ways of being that contribute to thriving and psychological health via small, consistent actions we can engage in each day. I love that the journal begins with compassion and self-care, providing the perfect foundation for a committed practice. And I now want to be a snail when I grow up (but you'll have to read the book to find out why)!"
—**Jill Stoddard, PhD,** author of *Be Mighty* and *The Big Book of ACT Metaphors,* and cohost of the *Psychologists Off the Clock* podcast

"In *ACT Daily Journal,* Diana Hill and Debbie Sorensen guide you on a journey of introspection, intention setting, and deliberate practice. Unlike many self-help books and guided journals, this book emphasizes *action.* Each day you will read (in only a few minutes!) about the rationale and science behind that day's practice. You will reflect on, and write in response to, a few prompts. Then you will weave throughout your day a simple practice. The result? In just eight weeks, you'll build mastery in the core processes of acceptance and commitment therapy (ACT), a complex and powerful therapy that can help you build a richer, more fulfilling life. Finally, a book that truly brings ACT to the masses!"

—**Alisha L. Brosse, PhD,** partner at the Boulder Center for Cognitive and Behavioral Therapies, and author of *End the Insomnia Struggle*

"Increasing your psychological flexibility is not a one-and-done issue. Like creating healthy patterns of eating, sleeping, or exercising, it's a one-day-at-a-time issue, and there is no better way to groove a daily habit of improvement than to keep a daily journal while you learn. This book will show you how, in a step-by-step, day-by-day, eight-week journey. You will be challenged but never overwhelmed; you will create new habits but never be bored. I highly recommend *ACT Daily Journal*."

—**Steven C. Hayes, PhD,** originator of ACT, author of *A Liberated Mind,* and foundation professor of psychology at the University of Nevada, Reno

"In this wonderful book, Diana Hill and Debbie Sorensen help readers use the tools of ACT to develop self-compassion and psychological flexibility in the best possible way, applying it in their lives. The authors create an engaging, immersive experience in which readers are gently guided through brief, easy-to-follow practices and reflections to help them work with life struggles and build lives filled with meaning, purpose, and kindness. Highly recommended!"

—**Russell Kolts, PhD,** professor of psychology at Eastern Washington University, and author of *CFT Made Simple* and *The Compassionate-Mind Guide to Managing Your Anger*

"Are you ready to get in the driver's seat of your life and take it to the next level? In *ACT Daily Journal,* Diana Hill and Debbie Sorensen take you on a journey to greater purpose, joy, and fulfillment. Grounded in psychology, this journal is filled with self-reflection journal prompts and daily practices that guide you toward deeper self-awareness and realignment with what matters most to you. By the end of this eight-week journey, you will have the tools and firsthand experience needed to show up more fully in your life, reach your goals, and overcome any obstacles you face along the way."

—**Robyn L. Gobin, PhD,** licensed psychologist, assistant professor of community health at the University of Illinois at Urbana-Champaign, and author of *The Self-Care Prescription*

"With relatable personal stories, moving vignettes, and digestible descriptions of the science, this unique journal gently guides individuals through one of the most powerful treatment approaches available for managing mental health and improving quality of life. It's an inspired and inspiring read you will want to buy for anyone and everyone you care about."

—**Yael Schonbrun, PhD,** assistant professor at Brown University, and cohost of the *Psychologists Off the Clock* podcast

"Living your values can be hard work. With this guided journal, Hill and Sorensen have created a useful and practical resource to apply evidence-based skills to everyday life. It is a charming, compassionate, and helpful resource for anyone trying to live a more vibrant and value-consistent life."

—**Dayna Lee-Baggley, PhD,** registered psychologist who provides clinical care for medical, surgery, and cancer care patients, and conducts research as an assistant professor in the faculty of medicine at Dalhousie University; and author of *Healthy Habits Suck*

"Hill and Sorensen's *ACT Daily Journal* makes a wonderful addition to the ACT literature for both novice and expert alike. ACT strategies to build psychological flexibility are engagingly taught within a doable structure alongside relatable and motivating authors' anecdotes. I enthusiastically recommend this guided *ACT Daily Journal* to my clinical colleagues for use with their clients as well as themselves!"
—**Debra L. Safer, MD,** associate professor in the department of psychiatry and behavioral sciences at Stanford University School of Medicine

"*ACT Daily Journal* is a flexible, step-by-step guide to living with greater life vitality, and a perfect addition to any professional's library! Weaving in personal stories, quotes, and metaphors to introduce the six core components of psychological flexibility, it is highly engaging, relatable, warm, and accessible. With each week focusing on a different process; and each day, one small practice; clients can readily integrate skills into their daily lives. Highly recommended!"

—Rhonda M. Merwin, PhD, associate professor at Duke University School of Medicine, peer-reviewed ACT trainer, and coauthor of *ACT for Anorexia Nervosa*

For my husband, Craig. I love you.

—Diana

For Piper, Hadley, and Easan, with love.

—Debbie

Foreword

The Joy, Pain, and Value of Practice

Aristotle once stated, "For the things we have to learn before we can do them, we learn by doing them." Practice means to put into action a behavior you would like to learn or change. Sounds simple enough. But as many of you know, practice also takes discipline. A much harder thing to put into practice! Nonetheless, these two are intimately entwined in the ever-evolving process of learning and growth.

As humans, we will experience our own measure of joy and pain. We will meet incredible challenges and wonderful times of peace. We will rise and fall in life as we encounter the unpredictable, often chaotic, and amazing experiences of being alive. Our journeys will have many winding roads and undeveloped paths. How you walk those paths will matter. When your journey is finished and you look back along the road you have traveled, will you have traveled it well?

There may be many ways to answer this question; perhaps you will find that it was hard and your journey ended with a feeling of being disappointed or "beat up" by life. Perhaps your journey was sweet, an attitude of optimism carrying you through to the end. Whatever the case of your journey, it will be filled with obstacle after obstacle. Life works like that. A deep valley, a ragged crevice, an overly wide and long sunbaked field: we do not, for the most part, get to choose which obstacles will be placed in our path. Given the inevitability of life, however, we can choose how we show up to the obstacles, bringing what matters most to bear with every hindrance we meet. This will be the stuff of your purpose, the stuff of your personal meaning. It will be the stuff that makes life worth living.

Here I am talking about your values and how you bring them to bear in your everyday journey. In the *ACT Daily Journal,* authors Diana Hill and Debbie Sorensen invite us to look at how we will practice our values in our everyday lives. How can we bring meaning to moments of joy and moments of pain? How will you approach the ragged crevice? The steep path? What intention will you bring to this journey? *ACT Daily Journal* invites us to bring a hallmark of well-being—psychological flexibility—to each and every moment of our existence. If we can practice with discipline the ability to be present, living more fully in the here and now; if we can disentangle from the stories our minds feed us that hinder our progress; if we can learn to take perspective on stepping into the many different views that can be explored on any journey; if we can be courageous—opening up to what we feel and sense—and then take that next step on the path with intention linked to values and commitment, we will build something. We will build something important, something powerful. A life created by you, lived in and moved through by you in the way that you intended. Loving, laughing, crying, struggling, being in pain, being in peace, creating, playing, building, progressing—tasting all that life has to offer. Truly showing up to life in all of its fullest moments.

Your way of being in the world will be defined by what you do. And as Aristotle said, we learn by doing. We must practice with discipline how to be present to and engage in what matters to us most. The journey is amazing, but it is also short. Let the *ACT Daily Journal* guide you forward, opening you to the possibilities and curiosities awaiting your arrival. So, prepare the ground that will help you face your inevitable challenges. And let this book guide you into a lifelong practice—a lifelong discipline such that when you turn and look back at your path, you can say, my journey to the grave was not fraught with actions of safety and work to preserve every inch of my body, never taking the courageous path. Instead, just as Hunter S. Thompson did, you can loudly proclaim, "Wow! What a Ride!"

—Robyn Walser, author of *The Heart of ACT*

Welcome

Painting the Golden Gate Bridge

There's a tale that Diana's dad used to tell her as a little girl: *It takes so long to paint the Golden Gate Bridge that as soon as the job is finished, the painter has to turn around and start all over again.*

In your life have you ever felt like that painter? Do you keep facing similar problems, get stuck painting the same spots, or get so busy painting you forget to take in the view? Do you struggle against the discomfort of it all or start wondering if you're cut out for the job? Or do you find yourself painting for endless hours without a sense of why it's even worthwhile or in what direction you should head?

Life can feel a lot like painting the Golden Gate Bridge. That's why we developed *ACT Daily*, an eight-week collection of daily practices to help you paint the bridge of your life more fully, with more vitality, and in line with your deepest personal values.

To find meaning on the bridge of your life, it's important to:
- Have compassion for yourself when you make mistakes
- Pause from time to time and take in the view around you
- Make room for discomfort when things get boring, hard, or scary
- Hold your thoughts lightly when they're discouraging or unhelpful
- Identify the parts of your life that matter most to you, and do your best at those parts
- Look toward the work ahead with a sense of direction and perspective
- Keep at it—day after day after day

ACT Daily will help you with these important tasks. Give yourself eight weeks to try it out, and you just might find that it helps you, as it has helped us and our clients, live more freely, with more meaning, and with a deeper understanding of your inherent humanity.

Psychological Flexibility: The Key to Psychological Health

Acceptance and commitment therapy (ACT, pronounced like the verb "to act") lies at the heart of this program. ACT is a modern, evidence-based approach that offers a unique perspective on well-being. You might think that therapy is about getting rid of "bad" thoughts and feelings and encouraging "good" ones. ACT is different. It helps you *make room* for uncomfortable thoughts and feelings—because not only is discomfort part of life, it's inherently linked to what you care most about (Hayes, Strosahl, and Wilson 2012).

Hundreds of research studies show that the ACT processes taught in this book are beneficial, not only if you're struggling with psychological distress, such as depression or anxiety, but also if you want to improve your relationships, develop healthier exercise and eating behaviors, cope better with pain or health conditions, or make positive changes in the world (Hayes 2019).

ACT's aim is to build your *psychological flexibility,* the ability to be aware of the thoughts and emotions you're having and be flexible, even when they are painful, so you can make conscious, values-driven choices. If you're psychologically flexible, you're less caught up in struggling with difficult thoughts, emotions, and urges, and you're free to act more in line with your values (Hayes 2019). And ultimately, when you're psychologically flexible you can keep moving in the direction of the things that really matter to you, even when you encounter challenges along the way. When you're psychologically flexible, you:

- Are present in the life you have
- Know what you care about and live in a way that's consistent with your values
- Accept and allow discomfort and pain instead of avoiding it
- Notice and unhook from unhelpful thoughts
- Connect with an observer self, one who can see your experience from many perspectives

- Take committed action toward what matters most in your life

The reality is that discomfort and pain are embedded in every fulfilling life. And you're *even more* likely to experience discomfort when you engage in activities that matter deeply to you. When you're psychologically flexible, though, you're able to fully engage in your life and, as our colleague Jill Stoddard (2019, 74) says, be "the Me you want to be," even when strong emotions and inevitable problems arise.

Psychological flexibility looks like:
- Starting a new relationship even if you fear vulnerability
- Making a change to pursue meaningful work even when it's intimidating
- Being a caring parent even when your child is pushing your buttons
- Moving your body even when your mind screams *I don't want to!*
- Taking meaningful action even when it's uncomfortable or exhausting

Psychological flexibility builds resilience.

In order to build a life that matters to you, it helps be able to respond effectively to life's natural stressors. Just as deep roots and flexible branches keep trees from falling over in windstorms, psychological flexibility will help you better withstand the turbulence of life by rooting you in your values and helping you be more flexible in your responses. Psychological flexibility also makes us more resilient as a human species. We need it now, more than ever. Our ability to flexibly adapt and collaborate compassionately is key to meeting the challenges of our communities and our planet (Biglan 2015).

Your Eight-Week Program to Psychological Flexibility and Health

ACT Daily will teach you the core processes that make up psychological flexibility. These ACT processes aren't psychological "tricks" but rather ways of *being* that contribute to thriving and psychological health. Just like an experienced cook who can make a stir-fry with whatever's in the fridge, once you learn these core processes you can apply them to any ingredient that shows up in your life! The processes are dynamic and interconnected, and they are enhanced when you engage in them with compassion. They're also meant to be lived out in your daily life. Like your physical health, your psychological health depends on the small, consistent actions you do daily. For each day of this journal you will build psychological flexibility by doing a set of simple exercises—some reading, some writing, and some experiential practices—that will help you learn the processes associated with psychological health.

The core ACT processes of being present, cognitive defusion, acceptance, perspective taking, values, and committed action together comprise psychological flexibility. These processes work together, centered around compassion for yourself and others, to build a more flexible, resilient, and meaningful *you!*

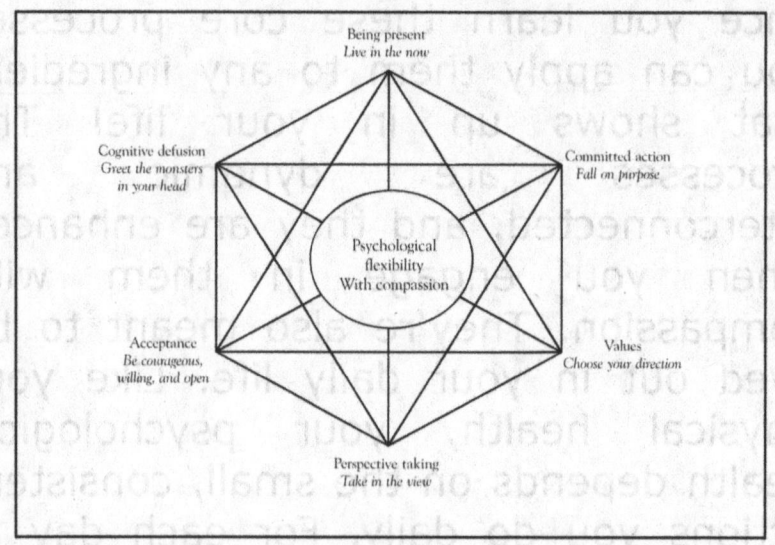

Week 1. Prepare the Ground

Often when we're trying to grow and learn something new, we get in our own way. If you're hyperfocused on your imperfections or neglect your self-care, you're less likely to make progress toward what really matters to you. During this week of focusing on compassion, self-care, and intention you will:

- Uncover the critical inner voice that keeps you stuck
- Cultivate a compassionate inner coach
- Learn how your brain's threat, drive, and caring systems influence

the degree to which you're critical or compassionate
- Develop simple self-care practices for emotional and physical well-being
- Learn to use your time with intention

Week 2. Being Present—Live in the Now

By becoming more aware of the present moment, you can fully experience your life as it's unfolding now and make more conscious decisions. During your week practicing *being present* you will:
- Move from living on autopilot to living with intention
- Savor more moments of your daily life
- Have greater self-awareness of your body's sensations, thoughts, and emotions
- Find a steady center in the face of difficulty
- Bring more awareness to your relationships and work

Week 3. Cognitive Defusion—Greet the Monsters in Your Head

Getting stuck in your own head is one of the biggest barriers to living life effectively. During this week, you will learn a process called *cognitive defusion*, which will help you:
- Notice your chatty mind
- Step back and create space from your thoughts
- Use humor and playfulness to get unstuck from thoughts
- Let go of trying to control your thoughts
- Get more flexible with rules, being right, and shoulds
- Pay attention to thoughts that are helpful, not harmful

Week 4. Acceptance—Courageous, Willing, and Open

Psychological flexibility means opening up to all aspects of your

emotional experience, even the unpleasant ones, in order to do the things that matter to you. During your week focusing on *acceptance* you will:
- Explore the messages you've been taught about emotions
- Recognize your avoidance strategies, such as numbing out, distracting yourself, turning down opportunities, or speeding through life
- Uncover the consequences of avoiding pain and discomfort
- Increase your willingness to face all of your emotions, thoughts, and sensations, pleasant and unpleasant alike

Week 5. Perspective Taking—Take In the View

The ability to shift perspective helps you open your mind beyond the stories it has about yourself, placing you on a grander, more flexible vantage point. During your week practicing *perspective taking* you will:
- Identify self-stories that keep you stuck

- Become more flexible with labels you assign to yourself
- Step into your "sky mind," a perspective that makes room for all of your inner experiences
- Zoom out and take perspective over time
- Explore broader possibilities in your life

Week 6. Values—Choose Your Direction

What brings you meaning, purpose, and vitality in your life? What do you really care about? And what type of person do you want to be? During your week focusing on *values* you will learn to:

- Identify what you want your life to be about
- Explore your values within important life domains, such as family, work, community, and health
- Realign with your values when you get off track
- Explore impermanence as a way to uncover what matters most to you

Week 7. Committed Action—Fall on Purpose

Committed action is the process of taking ongoing steps in the direction of our values, even when those steps are difficult. This week you will use the science of behavior change to:
- Increase your motivation to change using values
- Focus on the process of taking action, rather than on outcome
- Develop small achievable habits
- Explore obstacles to behavior change
- Create contexts, consequences, and a team to support your valued actions
- Develop a flexible and sustainable action plan

Week 8: Flexible Integration—Hive Mind

During the final week you'll put together all the processes you've learned. You'll experience how each of these processes inform and influence each other, like bees working together in a hive, to help you build your psychological flexibility. You'll fluidly move between them and apply them beyond yourself, *ACTing* daily to create a life you can feel proud of.

How to Use ACT Daily

ACT Daily is a guided journal. Many journals are focused on introspection and expressing thoughts and feelings. *ACT Daily* is different; in addition to developing such insight, you'll learn about the processes that make up psychological flexibility, so you can apply them in small ways, every day, to create a more vibrant life. We designed this journal to help you learn and practice actionable skills and develop daily habits to build psychological flexibility and take steps toward living a more vibrant life. Whether you are new to ACT, or have years of ACT experience, there's always room to strengthen your ability with its processes and apply them more regularly in your own life. On most days of this eight-week course you will:

- Read a short passage about that day's ACT process
- Do a brief guided writing exercise
- Try a brief exercise on the spot
- Write about ACT in your life (In each day's "ACT in My Life" section, you'll have space to note the main values you want to focus on for the day, jot down your daily goals, reflect on the day's reading passage, or write about your personal experience practicing ACT.)
- Learn a simple practice to try in your daily life

ACT Daily invites you to focus on each psychological flexibility process for seven days. Our aim is for you to do each day's reading and writing in about fifteen minutes and then practice the ideas in your daily life.

With our therapy clients, we've seen that psychological flexibility processes are only helpful if people use them regularly in their life. To really understand ACT, you can't just read and write about it; you have to put it into practice. Still, we know you're busy, and we are too. As you'll learn in Week 7 (on committed action), habits are more likely to stick if you keep them small and apply them consistently—and that's what we'll help you do.

Although consistency is important, so is flexibility. You can start this journal at the beginning and work your way through each week in order, or you can start with the process you want to work on first. Consistent practice is helpful, but if you skip some days now and then, or if it takes you longer than a week to work through a given process, don't sweat it. Just pick up where you left off and keep moving forward.

About Us

We are both clinical psychologists, cohosts and creators of the *Psychologists Off the Clock* podcast, and good friends who care a lot about values-based living. We share a value of using cutting-edge and effective ideas from psychology research to help our clients and others thrive in their daily lives.

ACT Daily is a culmination of what we have learned from years of academic study, interviewing more than 150 experts in the field of psychology, and thousands of hours of clinical practice. We've both trained extensively in several different forms of therapy and have found ACT to be the most helpful approach in our own lives and the lives of our therapy clients.

ACT Daily also draws heavily from our own personal fumbles and successes in using research-based principles from psychology in our own lives. As busy working parents, daughters, partners, and friends, we often struggle to put the ideas we've learned as psychologists into practice on a daily basis. Like everyone, we sometimes lose track of what's important, get stuck in our own thoughts and emotions, and get caught up in our day-to-day problems. Throughout this book, you'll hear our stories and learn how we've used these concepts ourselves to live more flexibly, and with more purpose. With a healthier mind, heart, and body, *ACT Daily* will help you live a more satisfying life. We hope you value the process of using *ACT Daily* as much as we valued creating it for you!

ACTing Daily: A Lifelong Process

In closing, it turns out that the story about the Golden Gate Bridge is only a tale; the painters don't start at one end, paint all the way through, and start over. In reality, a crew of painters works continually to maintain the bridge. And much like the painting of the bridge, engaging the processes of psychological flexibility is a lifelong endeavor.

The two of us have been practicing ACT for many years, both professionally and personally, and there's still more for us to learn and practice every day. We hope that even after you've finished this eight-week course you will continue to use ACT in your daily life. Consider this journal to be a maintenance handbook for when the paint starts chipping off your life, as it inevitably will. This journal can help you continue to live a values-driven life.

Week 1
Prepare the Ground

If you grow a vegetable garden, as we both do, you know that before you can start planting seeds, it's wise to tend to your soil. You want to create conditions that will help your plants grow, thrive, and be resilient in the face of inevitable challenges.

Similarly, when you embark on a new project that requires openness, time, and effort, such as *ACT Daily,* it helps to prepare yourself for the challenges that will arise. Perhaps you've started journals or self-help programs before, only to get stuck or to lose motivation and stop. This week, before you dive into the ACT processes of psychological flexibility, you'll prepare your soil with compassion, self-care, and intentional use of time.

Compassion

Compassion plays a key role in psychological well-being. Having compassion for yourself makes you more resilient during life's challenges, helps you stick to healthy habits, and enhances your compassion for others (Neff 2015). Having compassion for others forms the foundation of healthy relationships, caregiving, social justice, and a sense of purpose in life.

Compassion is an active, not passive, process. As Gilbert and Choden (2014, 105) define it, *compassion* is "a sensitivity to the suffering of oneself and others, combined with a commitment to do something about it." First, we become aware that someone (including ourselves) is hurting, then we move toward the hurt person and offer help. When practicing self-compassion, it helps to think of it as having three components, as outlined by researcher Kristen Neff (2015):

1. **Mindfulness:** Be fully present with your experience without judgment
2. **Kindness:** Be caring, gentle, and warm toward yourself when you're struggling

3. **Common humanity:** Understand that all humans are imperfect and suffer

Taking a kind stance toward yourself and others will make a big difference in your ability to tolerate distress, and it will help you to feel encouraged and to say yes to your deepest callings.

Living a values-driven life can be challenging and painful at times. Compassion can help you take meaningful action in the face of those challenges.

Real Self-Care

It takes inner resources to do the hard work of building a meaningful life. Tuning in and tending to your physical and emotional needs will help you keep at the important work of becoming more psychologically flexible.

Intentional Use of Time

Being intentional about your use of time will help you prioritize the things that are most important to you. In this chapter you'll take a look at how you're using your time and choose to organize it around activities you care most about.

Over the next eight weeks you'll build psychological flexibility by trying new things and relating to your thoughts and emotions in new ways. Preparing the ground this week will serve you well as you take on the important work ahead.

Date: _____

Day 1: Your Inner Critic

Diana: *When my son was six, he wanted to learn to surf. Though I grew up in Santa Barbara, I'd never tried surfing because I don't like taking risks or being cold. But I was practicing ACT, so I let my value of being an engaged parent win out over fear and shivers. During my first lesson, the instructor said, "Don't worry, I get five-year-olds and seventy-five-year-olds standing every time." When I fell try after try, you can predict where my mind went. What is wrong with me? Five-year-olds can do this! What I really needed was an encouraging voice to remind me I wasn't there to stand, but there to engage with my son. A compassionate voice that encouraged me to look to what I valued.*

What does your inner monologue sound like when you're trying something new or struggling? Are you harsh, judgmental, and negative in ways you'd never be toward someone else? Do you reject yourself?

We can be so hard on ourselves.
Curiously, we're often meanest to ourselves when we're most vulnerable, struggling, or stepping outside our comfort zone. In these moments, our inner critic tries to set things straight by being perfectionistic, setting high standards, and judging.

There are many reasons why we might be self-critical. We may have internalized the critical voices of caregivers, absorbed individualistic ideals such as "pull yourself up by your bootstraps," or internalized messages based in stereotypes, racism, or other people's standards. Self-compassion offers you a chance to choose a more reassuring voice—in the moments when you need encouragement most.

Today you'll identify your critical voice so that tomorrow you can start growing a more compassionate one.

ACT Daily Writing: Meet Your Inner Critic

Write about your inner critic. How has it shown up in your life? What did it say to you when you were younger? What about more recently?

_____
_____
_____
_____
_____
_____
_____

Write about something that's hard for you now. In what way does your inner critic show up when you are struggling? What does it say?

_____
_____
_____
_____
_____
_____

Try It Out: Feeding Your Inner Critic

Have you ever stopped to wonder what your critic wants? There is an ancient Tibetan practice called "feeding your inner demons" (Allione 2008). In this meditation, the practitioner personifies his or her inner demons, asks them what they're hungry for, and then imagines "feeding" them what they desire. Close your eyes and imagine that your inner critic is in front of you, personified. Ask these questions and notice what shows up:

Why are you here?

How are you trying to help me?

What do you need from me?

Become curious about your inner critic. What could satisfy its true hunger?

ACT in My Life: Today's Values, Goals, Reflections

_____
_____
_____
_____
_____
_____
_____

Today's Practice

Be on the lookout for your inner critic's voice today. When you spot it, approach it with curiosity.

Date: _____

Day 2: Fostering Self-Compassion

What if instead of being harsh with yourself when you're hurting, you had an inner coach who was kind, courageous, and forgiving? Today we're going to help you develop that compassionate inner coach, one who wants the best for you, cares for you, and supports you.

In ACT, you get to choose which thoughts you listen to. When your critic shows up, you can get stuck in its message, or you can disregard it and turn your attention to more helpful thoughts instead. Choosing the latter doesn't mean that your critic will go away, it just means you can be more flexible and compassionate in how you treat yourself and respond to your mind.

As Russell Kolts notes in episode 50 of our podcast, "When you really look at what it is like to have a human life, compassion is the only thing that makes sense" (2018). We couldn't agree more.

ACT Daily Writing: Your Compassionate Coach

In moments of struggle, what would you want your compassionate inner coach to say to you (e.g., *You are enough, I accept you exactly as you are, You're doing the best you can right now)?*

_____
_____
_____
_____
_____
_____

Try It Now: Compassionate Touch

Touch can be a powerful, nonverbal way to foster self-compassion. We use touch to soothe babies, express love to our partners, and let our friends know they are not alone. You can activate self-compassion by practicing caring touch with yourself now:

1. Place both of your hands over your heart and feel it beating.
2. Move one hand to your belly, keeping one hand on your heart. Take long, slow breaths.
3. Place your hands on your cheeks and hold your face as you would hold that of someone you love.

ACT in My Life: Today's Values, Goals, Reflections

_____
_____
_____
_____
_____

Today's Practice

Catch yourself during moments when you're beating yourself up. When you do, repeat one of the compassionate statements you noted above. As you say it, you may want to add a little caring touch, too, by placing your hands on your heart in a simple gesture of self-compassion.

Date: _____

Day 3: From Threat and Drive to Caring

Yesterday you began to practice self-compassion. You may have noticed that self-compassion led to feelings of contentment, connection, and well-being, or that it motivated you to be kinder toward others. That's because self-compassion activates an emotion system in your brain designed for affiliation and caring. Compassion-focused therapy (Gilbert 2014; Kolts 2016) describes humans as having three primary emotion systems with different functions:

The *caring system* regulates the way we take care of ourselves and others.

The *drive system* seeks out resources to help us survive and thrive.

The *threat system* picks up on threats and provokes strong emotions that motivate us to seek safety.

All three are necessary for survival, and ideally you want to find a helpful balance between them. Yet sometimes our threat and drive systems dominate our experience and override our caring system.

Debbie: *Sometimes I feel like my drive system is more like an overdrive system. I have a long to-do list and so many balls in the air that I can't juggle them all. Achieving more can feel good, but when I'm in overdrive mode, sometimes my drive system takes over and my caring system is nowhere to be found. When that happens, I feel overcaffeinated, unfocused, and disconnected from others. Now that I've learned about the three systems of emotion regulation, I've started noticing when I'm feeling this way and making a point of slowing down to get my systems back in balance.*

Today we'll draw from compassion-focused therapy to explore your threat and drive systems. Tomorrow we'll take a look at your caring system and how you can activate it with compassion.

ACT Daily Writing: Your Threat and Drive Systems

Your threat system motivates you to quickly avoid risks. When threatened, your body prepares to fight, flee, or freeze, you focus on danger, and you may feel anger, anxiety, or disgust. But when your threat system is chronically activated you can feel on edge, irritable, or stressed, or you may have difficulty sleeping.

What people, situations, or activities stimulate your threat system? What happens in your body? How do you behave? How dominant is this system now? What's activating it?

_____
_____
_____
_____
_____

The drive system motivates us to acquire food, seek shelter, position ourselves socially, and find a mate. When it's activated, you may feel excited or a sense of vitality. But when it's too dominant you may experience craving, overbusyness, competition, reduced empathy, or restlessness.

What people, situations, or activities stimulate your drive system? What happens in your body? How do you behave? How dominant is this system now? What's the cause?

_____
_____
_____
_____

ACT in My Life: Today's Values, Goals, Reflections

_____
_____
_____
_____
_____
_____
_____
_____
_____
_____

Today's Practice

Today, take note of your threat and drive systems. Notice your body sensations, thoughts, and actions related to them.

Date: _____

Day 4: Cultivate Compassion

Yesterday you took a look at your threat and drive emotion regulation systems. Today you're going to explore your caring system. As Paul Gilbert (2014) teaches, it's not our fault that we have "tricky" brains, but it is our responsibility to reorient our mind and behavior toward caring. You can mobilize your caring system through compassion.

Compassion can flow in three ways (Gilbert 2014):
1. Giving compassion to others
2. Receiving compassion from others
3. Giving compassion to ourselves

You can also activate your caring system through body-based soothing practices, such as gentle touch and slow, soothing breathing, or by imagining a time when you felt compassion for or from another. In caring mode, you have greater capacity to feel empathy for others, are more open-minded, and have more courage to engage in difficult, meaningful actions.

Diana: There's a business in my town called Cat Therapy. You can go there to cuddle and play with rescued cats, or you can fill out an application to take one home. It makes sense it's called "therapy"—what better way to soothe your nervous system than to give and receive compassion from a furry friend?

ACT Daily Writing: Your Caring System

Think of a time when you were struggling and received compassion from another person. What did this person say and do that was compassionate? Describe this person's tone of voice, body language, and facial expressions.

_____
_____
_____

Now think about a time when you gave compassion to someone who was struggling. What did you feel? What did you do to show compassion?

_____
_____
_____

Write about a struggle you're having now. What qualities of compassion, such as those you noted above, could you offer yourself?

_____
_____
_____

Try It Now: What's Your Balance Today?

On a scale from 0 (not at all) to 10 (all the time), how dominant are your three systems today?
My threat system _____
My drive system _____
My caring system _____

ACT in My Life: Today's Values, Goals, Reflections

_____
_____
_____
_____
_____
_____
_____

Today's Practice

What simple activity could you do today to activate more caring in your life? Remember the three ways that compassion flows? Consider these elements to jump-start your caring system:
1. **Give compassion to others:** smile at a stranger, cuddle with your pet, or reach out to someone you love who is struggling.
2. **Receive compassion from others:** discuss your worries with someone you trust, or visualize a

time when you felt safe, secure, and at peace with someone.
3. **Give compassion to yourself:** for example, practice soothing rhythm breathing (check out episode 89 of *Psychologists Off the Clock,* Hill 2019b), spend some time in nature, savor a nice cup of tea, or listen to music you enjoy.

Choose one of the above examples, or come up with one of your own, and try it today.

Date: _____

Day 5: Real Self-Care

There's so much talk about self-care these days that it can start to feel like yet another thing you aren't doing well enough. The term might evoke images of pedicures and long bubble baths. But, as self-care expert Robyn Gobin (2019) shares on our podcast, "Real self-care means asking yourself, *What do I need most right now on a soul level?*" Real self-care could mean:

- Taking a step toward a goal you've been putting off
- Asking for help
- Straightening out your finances
- Engaging in a creative outlet
- Setting relationship boundaries
- Making a change that will help your future self

And you can practice real self-care in many domains of your life, including work, relationships, health, intellectual pursuits, social activism, or spirituality. Ideally, self-care should be anchored in your values and should fill your soul.

Common myths about self-care are that it's indulgent or selfish and only for people with money to spare. In reality, neither plentiful time nor financial resources are required.

Debbie: *When I think about people going on yoga retreats or doing spa treatments for self-care, I have pangs of envy. That's just not going to happen in my life as it is now. It helps me to pause and think about what I can do, within my real life, to better care for myself. Even if I can't go to a spa, I can walk my dog, spend time with someone I love, get extra sleep, or take time to relax on the couch with a good book. I can make room to engage in self-care in many small ways.*

Today we're going to take an honest look at your life and what real self-care looks like for you, because, if we're going to care for others, it's important to care for ourselves.

ACT Daily Writing: My Real Self-Care

When you take good care of yourself, what do you do?

How do you neglect yourself? What is the impact on you?

If you were going to take better care of yourself this month, what would self-care look like in terms of your health, work, relationships, finances, intellectual pursuits, altruistic efforts, or spirituality? What could be your daily self-care practice?

ACT in My Life: Today's Values, Goals, Reflections

_____
_____
_____
_____
_____
_____
_____
_____

Today's Practice

Find one small (or big) way to practice self-care and prioritize doing it today. Be sure it's aligned with your values and is realistic for you in your life as it is.

Date: _____

Day 6: Physical Self-Care

Diana: *I have scoliosis, which means I was born with a crooked spine, and sitting for long periods of time can be painful. As a therapist who sits for hours, I've had to get creative—and unconventional—in order to care for my back. Sometimes I sit on the floor on cushions across from my clients, stretch during short breaks, and ask for walking meetings with my supervisee. A lot of days my back hurts, despite these efforts. But I take refuge in knowing that I am engaging in my value of caring for my body, even at work.*

ACT cofounder Dr. Kelly Wilson likes to ask workshop participants, "What kind of critter are you? And what does this kind of critter need?" Caring for your physical self means asking yourself what movement, food, and rest your body needs to best live out your values. These activities directly impact your mental health and how you function across life's domains. Today you're going to explore what it would mean to care for your body as you would care for someone you love.

On a busy day physical self-care can be as simple as noticing what your body needs in the moment: you're thirsty or need to use the restroom. Other days it may mean paying more attention to your need for movement, play, nutritious food, or sleep.

Dr. Rhonda Merwin encourages her clients to care for themselves the way a warm, attuned parent would (Merwin, Zucker, and Wilson 2019). A good parent is neither overly rigid nor overly permissive, but rather has reasonable expectations and boundaries. A good parent cares for you with small things—taking you to the doctor, suggesting you spend time outside, putting you to bed—every day.

ACT Daily Writing: Tending to Your Body

Are there ways you've been neglecting your body's physical needs? What changes might you consider to take better care of your body? If you were to tune in and tend to your body like a loving parent would, how would you care for you?

_____
_____
_____
_____

ACT in My Life: Today's Values, Goals, Reflections

_____
_____
_____
_____
_____
_____
_____
_____

Try It Now: Parenting Yourself

Imagine yourself as a warm, attuned parent with healthy goals and realistic expectations for the day. Imagine parenting yourself as a loving parent today.

Today's Practice

Find one small thing you can do to care for your body today. What does your body need to thrive? More rest? More movement? More fresh food? Whatever you choose to do, once you've done it, notice how it feels to really care for your body in this way.

Date: _____

Day 7: Intentional Use of Time

Carving out time to do the practices in *ACT Daily,* and making it a habit, can be a challenge. In our busy lives, finding even fifteen free minutes can be difficult. We can get lost in the flow of time, so it's important to check in with ourselves periodically to evaluate how we use our limited time resources.

Each new day offers an opportunity to be more intentional about how we use our time, and to engage in what matters most to us. It can be helpful each day to prioritize tasks and plan for the habits we'd like to develop. To learn how you are really spending your time, try keeping track of your time with a time log (Vanderkam 2018). Once you look at your patterns, you might be surprised that you're spending hours each week doing things that aren't important to you.

We aren't saying that you need to be busy or productive every minute of the day. Indeed, downtime can be one of the best uses of time! But it's one thing to deliberately rest and quite another to let hours pass without noticing that you've been scrolling around online and missing out on doing the things you care most about.

Take an honest look at what you're really doing with your time. What would it be like to spend more time doing the things that matter most?

Debbie: *I sometimes think that I'm so busy I don't have enough time to read fiction anymore, even though it's one of my greatest joys in life. Keeping a time log helped me see that I actually spend plenty of time reading, but I'm reading " junk food"—scrolling around news and social media sites on my phone. If I really care about reading fiction, I can choose to put my phone down and spend time with a good book instead.*

ACT Daily Writing: Your Ideal Day

Imagine a day when you get to choose how you spend your time. Who would you spend time with and what would you do?

_____
_____
_____

ACT in My Life: Today's Values, Goals, Reflections

_____
_____
_____
_____
_____
_____
_____
_____

Today's Practice

In the space below, or on a separate paper or spreadsheet, keep a simple log of how you spend time today. At the end of the day, compare the log with the ideal day you wrote about above. Are you using time in ways that feel meaningful to you?

Wake-up time: _____

_____
_____
_____
_____
_____
_____
_____
_____
_____
_____
_____
_____
_____
_____
_____

Time to bed: _____

Final Reflections

Congratulations on completing your first week of *ACT Daily!* This week's work helped prepare your soil for planting the seeds of psychological flexibility. Take a moment to skim through the weeks ahead and decide where you want to go next. Pick your next chapter, and we'll meet you there!

Week 2

Being Present—Live in the Now

Technology, information overload, and fast-paced living all compete for a limited resource: *our attention.* We often live in a state of distraction, with our thoughts drifting from the future, to the past, to the future again. When our minds are pulled away from what we're doing here and now, as they are much of the time (Killingsworth and Gilbert 2010), it can start to feel like we're missing out on living—because we are. In this state we're living on autopilot, reacting to events without paying much attention.

With practice, you can step back, notice what's happening now, and, with greater awareness, make more intentional, deliberate choices. The ACT psychological flexibility process of being present puts you at the center of your own experience. Based on principles that can be traced back thousands of years to many of the world's religious traditions, being present increases your awareness of your thoughts, emotions, and behaviors. This will help you act less habitually and mindlessly and allow you to make more conscious, intentional choices in this moment.

Diana: *When I was a little girl and someone asked what I wanted to be when I grew up, I would say, "a snail." I liked that snails get to have their homes on their backs and are happy moving at their own pace. As I got older, I gave up on becoming a snail and instead thought I'd find happiness in graduating from school, getting married, or having another child. I found myself rushing to get to the next place before I could settle in. But as soon as I achieved one goal, a new one came along. Being present helps me see that right now is my home. I get to be what I've always wanted—a snail, with a home on my back wherever I go.*

Recent research (e.g., Goleman and Davidson 2017) suggests that paying attention to the present moment can help us:

- Be more resilient during times of stress
- Focus our attention
- Have more compassion for others
- Decrease inflammation and improve health
- Improve longevity markers

Being present, also known as mindfulness, has a strong body of research showing that it's beneficial in treating chronic pain, addiction, depressive relapse, and anxiety (Kabat-Zinn, Lipworth, and Burney 1985; Kabat-Zinn et al. 1992; Teasdale et al. 2000; Witkiewitz et al. 2013).

A formal meditation practice is a great way to strengthen your mindfulness skills, but it is not a requirement for practicing ACT (Wilson and DuFrene 2009). Instead, ACT emphasizes bringing awareness to your life as you are living it. You can practice being present by sitting quietly on a cushion, or you can practice it in your daily life while cooking breakfast, taking a shower, or stuck in traffic late for work!

This week, we offer you a series of stepping-stones to help you be more aware in the present moment. You'll take a look at where you could use a little more awareness, practice building new skills, and bring awareness to the areas that matter most to you.

Date: _____

Day 1: Autopilot

Debbie: *True confession: on weekdays, I sometimes eat breakfast in the car while driving to work ... while also listening to a podcast. I've been driving for more years than I care to admit, so I can arrive safely without much effort. I've eaten so many meals in this manner that I can chew my almond-butter toast and barely notice it. Clearly a person cannot pay attention to the road, a podcast, and one's food at the same time. So, I often arrive at work with little memory of my meal or of the drive itself. I wonder what I might have noticed had I paid more attention.*

We can do many routine things, such as eating and driving, without much thought. Although autopilot mode can be a useful shortcut, when we don't pay attention to what we're doing, we can miss out on the moment-to-moment events that make up our lives. Living on autopilot can also lead to automatic, unhelpful habits. We might automatically reach for the phone every time we're bored, or automatically pour ourselves a glass of wine at the end of the workday, whether we actually want one or not. It can start to feel like we are living in a fog, just going through the motions without being tuned in. As a yoga teacher once told Diana, "If you're wondering what is missing in your life ... it just might be you!"

Being present can help us be more tuned in to what's happening and to choose our actions more deliberately. By tuning in to the present moment, we can become less scattered, even when life is moving at a fast pace, and find a steady center from which to face life's challenges.

ACT Daily Writing: From Scattered to Engaged

In what situations do you tend to rush through tasks, live on autopilot, or feel scattered?

_____
_____
_____
_____
_____
_____
_____

With which people, activities, and moments would you like to be more present and engaged?

Try It Now: Today's Attention

Look at your agenda for today. Which events would you like to experience with your full attention and focus?

_____
_____
_____
_____
_____
_____

ACT in My Life: Today's Values, Goals, Reflections

_____
_____
_____
_____
_____
_____
_____
_____
_____
_____

Today's Practice

Today, bring awareness to your distractible mind. Without trying to change your thoughts, see if you can catch yourself rushing, scattered, or disengaged from one of the important events you listed above. Make a goal of catching yourself as many times as possible. Every time you do, you're strengthening the powerful process of being present.

Date: _____

Day 2: Beginner's Mind

Often, we move through life with the lens of *I already know. I already know* what my house, my family, or my town looks like, so why take another look? What gets lost in *already knowing* is noticing the intricacies of the present. Beginner's mind is the skill of experiencing something as if you've never done it or seen it before (McKay, Wood, and Brantley 2019). What am I seeing? Hearing? Feeling? With beginner's mind, you pay attention to things without preconceptions.

Diana: *A while back I paid to shovel someone else's mulch. I was on a retreat with biomechanist Katy Bowman learning about how to build more movement into my life during simple daily tasks. Under normal circumstances I would have prejudged shoveling mulch as drudgery, a chore. But approaching it with beginner's mind helped me see it as an opportunity to move my body! And, shoveling with a* *group of others had the added benefit of connection.*

Using beginner's mind in life is like wiping off a dirty windshield. You see things that you were missing in your life in real time, as opposed to how your mind has predetermined them to be.

For example, Diana often asks clients who struggle with restrictive eating to approach meals with beginner's mind. She suggests they imagine that they've never had the food in front of them before and to eat it as if it were the first time. Clients often report that their newfound awareness increases their willingness to branch out to new foods.

ACT Daily Writing: Start Where You Sit

Take a look around and pretend you've never seen the room you're sitting in. Look for details you might not have noticed or appreciated. Bring a sense of wonder to this space and write about what you see with fresh eyes. Where else might you want to use beginner's mind today?

_____
_____
_____
_____
_____
_____

Try It Now: Begin with Your Body

Often when we look at our body, we see flaws and make judgments (good and bad). Let's try something different. Next time you're in the bathroom, take a minute to look in the mirror at your eyes—as if you've never seen them before. Look at the colors in your irises, your eyelashes, your tear ducts. If you have longer than a minute, move to other parts of your face, and if you want, even to a body part that you judge harshly. What happens if you approach this body part with beginner's mind?

ACT in My Life: Today's Values, Goals, Reflections

_____
_____
_____
_____
_____
_____
_____
_____

Today's Practice

Use beginner's mind today. Enter your day as if you have never seen it before.

Date: _____

Day 3: Savoring Daily Life

Debbie: For many years I specialized in providing therapy for people with disabilities and chronic health conditions. Some of my clients had difficulty performing basic activities without assistance or specialized equipment. For instance, putting on socks or cutting food with a knife can be challenging for people who suddenly lose hand function. People often express feelings of loss over activities they previously thought were mundane. Often, we take the simplest things—the tasks we do every day without thinking about them—for granted.

Every day, many small moments pass us by. For example, when COVID-19 hit, many of us quickly began longing for the simple things that were put on hold—hugging friends, watching our kids play freely with their friends, and pouring cups of tea for neighbors. We realized how easily we overlooked things we loved about life because we hadn't been paying much attention to them. Had we known these activities would be taken away from us, we might have approached them differently.

Not only do we easily overlook happy moments, but the moments that catch our attention aren't always the ones we want to focus on. Our brain is designed to dismiss positive experiences and to pay attention to the negative ones—this keeps us safe and can help us to survive.

The good news is that you can enrich your life by intentionally savoring the experiences that matter to you. Do you want to savor feelings of contentment and connection? Gratitude and joy? According to Rick Hanson (2018), intentionally practicing awareness by savoring positive feelings that arise actually sculpts the neural structure of our brain! Our positive experiences are more likely to be transferred to our long-term memory when we linger on them and absorb them more fully.

ACT Daily Writing: Appreciating Daily Life

What moments of life do you take for granted? What moments might you savor or linger over in your daily life? What might you appreciate just a little bit more?

_____
_____
_____
_____
_____

Try It Now: The Small Things

Think about your day ahead. Imagine this was the last time you were going to engage in your daily activities (washing your face, greeting coworkers in person, cutting with a knife). Which aspects of your day would you want to linger on and appreciate just a little bit more?

ACT in My Life: Today's Values, Goals, Reflections

_____
_____
_____
_____
_____
_____
_____
_____

Today's Practice

Today practice savoring small enjoyable moments, to encode them in your memory. When you notice one, use the beginner's mind skill from Day 2 to see it with fresh eyes and to absorb it more fully.

Date: _____

Day 4: Embodiment

Diana: *My graduate research was in appetite awareness training for eating disorders. It can be a long journey to find and trust your satiety cues when you have repeatedly overridden them. I'd ask clients to explore:* What am I really hungry for? What does satisfaction feel like to me? Is this hunger or anxiety? Anger or fullness? *As clients rediscovered their body's callings and needs, they also found a deepened inner knowing. When you listen to your body, you can hear its wisdom.*

Take a look inside and you'll find a varied landscape of sensations, such as hunger, emotions, breath, and physical pain. Your body sends you signals all day long to help you reach homeostasis, or a state of balance. But we often discount or ignore these cues. As a baby you were naturally tuned in to your body. But over time you likely learned to focus more on your external world.

As adults we become increasingly detached from our body:
- Do you squelch your satiety signals with dieting or overeating?
- Do you mask your tiredness with caffeine?
- Do you quiet your aches and pains with substances?
- Do you spend so much time in your head that you forget you have anything below the neck?

It's not helpful to spend every minute focused on your body, but if you repeatedly cut yourself off from your body, you miss out on its rich information. And sometimes your attempts to control your body's cues can backfire.

Today you're going to bring awareness to your body's inner sensations, increasing what is called embodiment.

ACT Daily Writing: Tuning In

Are you connected to your body, or do you spend most of your time living in your head? How do you mask or ignore your body's inner signals? Are there negative consequences when you disconnect from your body?

_____
_____
_____
_____

Now, turn your attention inward. Notice your level of hunger, physical aches and pains, tension, and fatigue. Write about these sensations. What is your body asking for right now?

_____
_____
_____
_____

ACT in My Life: Today's Values, Goals, Reflections

_____
_____
_____
_____
_____
_____
_____

Today's Practice

Let's focus on increasing your awareness of your body, and your experience of living in it. Choose one of the following exercises:
- Set your phone alarm to go off at three random times today, and when it does ask yourself, *What's happening in my body?*
- Go barefoot outside, noticing the sensation of walking on different textures, such as that of grass, rocks, or dirt.

- Use appetite awareness training (Craighead 2006) to check in with your hunger and fullness each time you eat today. Before eating make a note of how hungry you are on a scale from 0 (very hungry) to 7 (very full). Rate your appetite again after eating.
- Pay attention to your breath. Notice where your breath moves in your body, its rhythm and the places where it pauses. Or, try out the ten-minute breathing meditation featured in episode 81 of *Psychologists Off the Clock* (Hill 2019a).

Date: _____

Day 5: Noticing Your Mind

Have you ever been so preoccupied while showering that you couldn't remember whether you shampooed? Or been so busy thinking about your to-do list while listening to the radio that you missed a whole news story? Minds love to comment nonstop. When you're busy worrying, analyzing problems, or replaying memories, you can lose track of what's happening right before your eyes.

Debbie: *A few years ago, I offered an ACT training in Salt Lake City. After checking into my hotel I walked to get dinner. My mind was busy thinking about the material to review, fretting about travel logistics, and problem solving where to find a decent dinner in an unfamiliar city. I had walked about two blocks before I looked up and noticed a beautiful snow-covered mountain range right in front of me! Often, life is like that; we're so preoccupied by the content of our* thoughts that we don't see what's right in front of us.

Even ACT trainers are mindless sometimes. Left unchecked, our mind tends to wander to almost anything but the things we're doing. That's not all bad. Sometimes your mind needs to roam free to rest; our mind gets fatigued by sustained, focused attention. Mind wandering can lead to creativity (Preiss et al. 2016), and if your mind wanders to an engaging topic your mood may even improve (Franklin et al. 2013). But if you're chronically distracted, you'll likely miss out on important moments.

The first step in changing your relationship with your mind is becoming aware of it. If you notice your thought patterns, they can't push you around as much. Let's start by building awareness of your thoughts.

ACT Daily Writing: Today's State of Mind

Write about the quality of your mind today. Is it busy? Slow? Calm? Scattered? Clear? Notice your urge to write *the content* of what you're thinking. For now, just describe its *quality*.

_____
_____
_____
_____
_____

Try It Now: Running Commentary

Time yourself for one minute. Write down all your thoughts. When you're done, step back and observe the *content* of your mind.

_____
_____
_____
_____
_____
_____

ACT in My Life: Today's Values, Goals, Reflections

_____
_____
_____
_____
_____
_____
_____
_____

Today's Practice

Sometimes being silent can help us tune in to our present experience. For example, at Thich Nhat Hanh's monastery in France, the monks and nuns encourage engaging in "noble silence" from dinner through breakfast. Noble silence is seen as an opportunity to not *have to* talk, so people can be more aware of their minds, their bodies, and the present moment. Today, try eating a meal, taking a walk, or sitting outside in noble silence. Notice the quality and content of your mind, your thoughts, and the world around you.

Date: _____

Day 6: Emotional Awareness

Debbie: Once, I had to have a conversation at work that I expected to be difficult and unpleasant. As the conversation approached, I noticed I was putting up my emotional guard, bracing myself, and wanting to get it over with. When I became aware of my thoughts and feelings, I changed course. I made a conscious decision to be genuine and open and to approach the conversation with courage. The conversation ended up being a meaningful one. Had I not first noticed my thoughts and emotions by being present, that wouldn't have been the case.

When you're tuned in to your emotional experience, it's easier to show up in a way that's wholehearted—authentic, open, and able to approach with courage even the things that scare you. Most people feel many different emotions throughout the day, and this is no accident. Fear keeps us alive, moral emotions like shame can help bond us to others, happiness can motivate us, and sadness means we care.

Emotions are complex. They're linked to thoughts and memories and can include strong sensations and urges to act. Some emotions last only a few seconds, others a few minutes; and when they last longer than that, they can become moods. Many of us are often unaware of our own emotions because we've spent a lifetime tuning them out, or pushing them away. For example, you might:
- Turn to your phone or snacks when you're stressed
- Feel vaguely uncomfortable inside, but struggle to understand your discomfort
- Start a fight with your partner, not realizing you're feeling hurt

Increasing emotional awareness and really opening up to the emotions you feel will help build psychological flexibility. You'll also grow your emotional intelligence, which helps you better empathize with others, communicate effectively, and be a stronger leader (Goleman 2005). Over time you'll learn to approach your emotions with acceptance, see them as a source of information, and make choices directed by your values instead of reacting with little awareness.

ACT Daily Writing: What Are You Feeling?

Describe what you're feeling right now. Where in your body do you feel your emotions? What are their sensations? What urges, images, or memories are associated with how you're feeling?

_____
_____
_____
_____
_____
_____

Try It Now: Physicalizing Emotion

Pick one of the emotions you wrote about above. Explore it. Where do you feel it in your body? Does it feel heavy or light? Is it moving around? Does it feel cold or hot to you? What sensations do you notice inside?

ACT in My Life: Today's Values, Goals, Reflections

_____
_____
_____
_____
_____
_____
_____
_____
_____
_____

Today's Practice

Choose an activity, something you care deeply about, and show up wholeheartedly today. As you go about this task, open up to your emotions by feeling them in your body and staying fully present.

Date: _____

Day 7: Being Mindful Where It Matters

We've been building awareness for an important reason: to help you make your life as meaningful as possible. This is where being present meets values (see Week 6). But we don't expect (or even want) you to be 100 percent present every moment of the day. Instead, work on being more aware and engaged where it counts—such as in your relationships and at work.

Diana: *I often give my partner couples therapy retreats as "Homer gifts" (like when Homer Simpson gives Marge a bowling ball with an H on it). On one retreat, we learned about "sliding door moments," opportunities to step toward or away from our partners (Gottman and Silver 2013). In these moments, marriages are strengthened or weakened. I realized how often I failed to step* *through the sliding door. A typical example:*

Diana's spouse: *"Honey, check out that red-tailed hawk."*

Diana: *"Hold on, I need to schedule this client."*

To be emotionally responsive and receptive in our relationships we must see and hear our loved ones with our whole being. When your friend is going through a breakup, listening fully is more soothing than giving advice. When your children are hurt, holding them is more healing than rushing for an ice pack. And when your partner tells you there's a hawk outside, it's a good idea to take a look.

Work is another area where showing up mindfully can be hard. We spend a lot of time doing work—jobs, domestic work, and other productive activities. When we have a stressful interaction, or an unpleasant task, we might be tempted to get angry, disengage, or procrastinate.

Being present in relationships and work is a lot like high-intensity interval training; even short spurts of effort will have a big impact on your psychological flexibility!

ACT Daily Writing: More Mindful in Love and Work

Write down the people who really matter to you. How do you miss their bids for attention? How can you show up more wholeheartedly? What's one thing you can do today to be more present with those you love?

_____
_____
_____
_____
_____

What about your work? How can you show up more fully? When do you tend to be unfocused or unproductive? How might you be more present at your work today?

ACT in My Life: Today's Values, Goals, Reflections

_____
_____
_____
_____
_____
_____
_____
_____

Today's Practice

Today, practice being present with someone you love, with work, or with something else that matters to you.

Notice when your attention moves away and bring it back over and over again.

Final Reflections

This week you practiced being more aware in the present moment. You moved from living on autopilot to developing a beginner's mind that savors the fullness of this moment as it unfolds in your body, emotions, and mind. You'll find that the ACT process of being present is woven into every week of this journal. If you choose to move on to unhooking from your thoughts next (Week 3), or another ACT process, bring your beginner's mind with you!

Week 3

Cognitive Defusion—Greet the Monsters in Your Head

Diana: When my oldest child was three, there was a period of time when he woke in the night seeing monsters in his room. My initial instinct was to tell him what most parents would: "Honey, there's no such thing as monsters." But, as an ACT therapist, I taught him to instead greet the monsters. "What do the monsters look like? Where are they in the room? What do you think they want from you?" And when he told me he thought the monsters were hungry, we made them a bowl of cereal. After a few nights of leaving cereal outside his door, the monsters didn't wake him anymore. Apparently, they were full.

You've probably woken in the night with your own version of monsters in your head. Maybe you've been hooked by worries about the future, a work problem, or a relationship concern. Just like trying to rationalize with a kid about monsters, trying to rationalize with your mind at 2a.m. rarely works.

Your middle-of-the-night thinking comes from being human. Your brain has the unique ability to create language, which allows you to think, plan, imagine, and make meaning. But language is a double-edged sword. With language you can worry, ruminate, create rules, and judge. It's normal to get caught up in convincing thoughts, or to want to stop yourself from thinking—especially when your thoughts are distressing. But both of these strategies can backfire. Have you noticed that problem solving in the middle of the night only amplifies your worry? Or that trying not to think about your problem only makes you think about it more? According to thought-suppression research in psychology (Wegner et al. 1987), the more we attempt to get rid of unwanted thoughts, the stronger they rebound. If you have social anxiety, you know how this works. The more you try to not think about how awkward you are with another person, the more your mind points out *I'm being so awkward right now!*

Language also allows your mind to make comments about yourself and the world around you—*all day long.* Even as you read this, your mind has something to say. It may not even be related to what you're reading! Not only is your mind never quiet, it tends to focus on the negative. As Rick Hanson (2020b) shared on episode 122 of our podcast, our brain is like Teflon for positive experiences and Velcro for negative ones. For evolutionary reasons, the negative thoughts we have tend to stick; the positive thoughts, we can't get to stick around at all.

When you're caught up in either fighting or believing your mind's chatter, you become what ACT calls *cognitively fused.* There's no space between *you* and the thoughts your mind is generating. Cognitive fusion entangles you in your thoughts, which makes it hard for you to see your experience, and yourself, clearly.

Are You Cognitively Fused?

Answer these questions to see how fused you are with your thoughts:

Do you have a hard time paying attention and get distracted by your thoughts?

Do you believe your thoughts are facts, and follow your mind's rules and shoulds?

Do you believe your mind's judgments about yourself and others?

Do you let your thoughts direct your behavior without second-guessing their helpfulness?

Is it hard for you to separate yourself from the thoughts you have?

If you answered yes to most of the questions above, congratulations! You are human.

Like most humans you probably try a number of things to quiet the thoughts that bother you most. Perhaps you try to think "happy thoughts," make your mind go blank, or avoid things that remind you of your monsters. Yet you probably noticed that when you automatically follow your thoughts, they can take you off track. And, when you resist your thoughts they keep coming back. What else can you do?

Defuse from your thoughts! Cognitive defusion is different from trying to challenge or stop your thinking. Rather, it involves relating to your thoughts differently. You take an observational stance with your thoughts and recognize *I am the one watching this, and I am not these thoughts.* By spending less time being hooked by your thoughts you're freed up to move more flexibly toward what really matters to you. This week you'll practice cognitive defusion when you:

- Notice your nonstop chattering mind
- Step back and look at your thoughts instead of being stuck in them
- See how attempting to control your wild and wacky thoughts can backfire
- Shift away from behavior that's inflexibly governed by judgments,

shoulds, and rules and toward behavior that's flexibly guided by your values
- Attend and respond to thoughts that help you act the way you want to be in the world

We hope you'll get a little distance from, and perspective on, the monsters in your head. And once you have more space from your thoughts, you'll be more able to choose which thoughts are worth your attention.

Date: _____

Day 1: Your Chatty Seatmate

Imagine you're unhappily settling into a middle seat on a long, cross-country flight and find yourself stuck next to an airplane chitchatter. Your seatmate for the next five hours talks nonstop. He complains, criticizes you, judges the airline, and forecasts doom and gloom ahead. At first, you try to ignore him, putting on headphones, but he still won't stop talking. Then you get annoyed and argue back, even telling him to please be quiet, and he *still* won't stop! So, you distract yourself with the in-flight magazine, and even order an overpriced cocktail to numb out from this experience. But no matter what you do, you're stuck with him.

Guess what! You have a chatty seatmate with you all the time—your mind! Your mind narrates your life and rarely stops chatting. And sometimes that chatter consists of unhelpful thinking that's very hard to ignore.

What can you do instead? Allow your chatty seatmate to talk without getting so caught up in what he's saying. Don't let him push you around. Shift your attention to things you care more about. Become a skillful observer who acts based on your values, not on what your seatmate dictates. Just as the excruciatingly long flight detailed above eventually passes, so, too, does every moment in your life.

ACT Daily Writing: Your Mental Chatter

Write about what your mind has been chattering about today. What are some of the comments your mind is making about you, your future, the world around you? Which of these comments are helpful (those you want to listen to)? Which are unhelpful (those you want to disregard)?

Try It Now: Brush Your Teeth

Get up and brush your teeth. Do it even if you already brushed your teeth today. Your dentist will thank you. While you're brushing, notice how your mind chatters about anything but teeth brushing. Notice your mind complain, comment, and plan, just like the chatty seatmate on the airplane. Can you notice that chattering mind, but not get hooked by it? Can you also look at your teeth in the mirror or focus on getting all those hard-to-reach spots? Focus on brushing your teeth with intention, letting your chatty seatmate become background noise.

ACT in My Life: Today's Values, Goals, Reflections

_____
_____
_____
_____
_____
_____
_____
_____
_____
_____

Today's Practice

Pay special attention to your mind, the chatty seatmate. Pick one task you are doing today (such as showering, dressing, or eating) and notice the thoughts that show up without getting hooked by them. Be on the lookout for the real doozies—the thoughts that trip you up and pull you away from the task at hand. Can you notice these thoughts while also bringing attention to what you care about in this task?

Date: _____

Day 2: Thriller or Slapstick?

Have you ever gotten really stressed out watching a suspenseful movie? But then you remembered it's not real—that you're actually sitting in your living room with a bowl of popcorn on your lap? As in a movie, our minds can manipulate us into believing something that isn't real; however, if you can look at your thoughts from a distance and see them for what they are—that the blood on the screen is really ketchup—your mind is less likely to push you around. Now and then, it's helpful to step back from your mind, label your thoughts as thoughts, and notice what's happening in the moment.

Diana: *I mustered the energy to get to yoga class one time only to find myself in line behind a couple buying a yoga package. I had cut it close, and class was starting soon. Meanwhile, the couple was going back and forth about vacation plans and work schedules. As time ticked by, my mind complained and judged:* It took a lot to get here, *and now I'm stuck—just standing here! Finally, the couple finished, and I got to class, only to find the teacher demonstrating mountain pose—a pose in which you just stand there!*

Often we're so caught up in our thoughts we don't notice them for what they are. It's amazing how much thoughts can taint the experience of life! What if you had a more playful relationship with your thoughts? Appreciating them as expressions of your wondrous—and sometimes obnoxious—mind, rather than letting them carry you away? Today you'll gain awareness of your thoughts—and relate to them in a playful new way.

ACT Daily Writing: Your Movie Mind

Sometimes it helps to not take our thoughts so seriously. Imagine watching your mind like you would watch a movie. What thoughts and imagery are particularly captivating nowadays? What worry, regret, and criticism scripts are you caught in?

_____
_____
_____
_____
_____
_____

Try It Now: Cast Your Mind

Now think about the characters of your mind's movie. Does your mind have a regular cast, such as Regretful Roger or Never-Good-Enough Nelly? What would you name your cast?

_____
_____

What would today's main character be named? What would this character wear and what's her script? Examples:

Diana's mind: *Overcontrolling Ophelia, wearing a pressed shirt buttoned to the top, nagging, "You aren't doing enough."*

Debbie's mind: *Preoccupied Penelope, disheveled, talking fast, rattling off a to-do list repeatedly.*

Your Mind: _____

_____

_____

ACT in My Life: Today's Values, Goals, Reflections

_____
_____
_____
_____
_____
_____
_____
_____
_____

Today's Practice

As you go through your day today, step back from your thoughts. Catch unhelpful scripts or familiar mind characters. Instead of being engrossed in thoughts, notice them for what they are: thoughts playing out scenes in your mind.

Date: _____

Day 3: Wild and Wacky Thoughts

Debbie: *A few years back, I briefly (and unsuccessfully) tried eating fewer carbs. One day at lunch, I saw a baked potato in the cafeteria and told myself, I can't eat that potato, it has carbs. Guess what happened. I spent the rest of the day obsessing about the baked potato and telling myself to stop thinking about it. The more I told myself to stop thinking about it, the more I couldn't help it. Every minute or so, I pictured that potato. If I had just allowed myself to think freely about that boring old baked potato, perhaps it wouldn't have turned into something so big in my head that day!*

The mind can be wild sometimes. You tell it not to think about a baked potato, and what does it do? Thinks about a baked potato all day long. Even if we can suppress our thoughts for a while, they come rebounding back stronger than ever. We've all gotten well-meaning advice about thinking, such as "Don't worry!" or "Just don't think negative thoughts." On the surface, this seems helpful. There's just one problem: such advice doesn't work. Minds don't like to be controlled.

Not only that, minds can be wacky! If we told you we were going to attach a bullhorn to your head and broadcast all your thoughts and mental images, how would you feel? Embarrassed? Mortified? Us too. We may worry that we're the only ones having these kinds of thoughts, or even that we're going crazy, but we *all* have weird, wacky thoughts sometimes. And thoughts are only a problem when we buy into them or try to control them.

ACT Daily Writing: Mind Control

Write about a time in the past when you tried to control your mind or think positive thoughts. How successful were your efforts in the long run?

How about now? Are there topics you try not to think about? How well is that working?

Try It Now: Just Don't Think

We have a challenge for you. Try not thinking about your big toes while you read the rest of this passage. Force yourself not to notice them. You can think of anything else you want, just not that tingly feeling in your big toes. Could you do it?

Now, for a minute, let your mind roam free. Loosen up on efforts to control your thoughts. What do you notice?

ACT in My Life: Today's Values, Goals, Reflections

_____
_____
_____
_____
_____
_____
_____
_____
_____
_____

Today's Practice

Today, be on the lookout for two things: first, wacky thoughts that pop into your mind (the ones you wouldn't want to broadcast through a bullhorn), and second, times that you try to control your thoughts by clearing out your mind or by changing your thoughts. Reflect on your attempts to control your mind.

Date: _____

Day 4: Your Inner Judge

Debbie: *One Halloween, while trick-or-treating with kids, my neighbor and I got into a debate over which is better, sour candies or peanut butter cups. (I mean, sour candies? Really?) I noticed we both stated our opinions about fruity versus chocolate candy as if they were facts. "No way! Peanut butter cups are so much better." Do you see how this opinion is stated as fact?*

The human mind is *great* at making quick evaluations. This ability helps us make decisions and stay safe. For example, if you see a cockroach at a sushi place, you might benefit from judging it as "disgusting" and making other dinner plans. Sometimes our judgments are accurate.

The problem is that sometimes our assumptions are wrong because we don't have enough information. What's more, we often confuse judgments for facts. For example:

She's such a good girl.

My anxiety is the worst.

His car is nicer than mine.

These statements are opinions presented as truths. When we present something as a truth, we lose sight of how perspective and context are shaping our thoughts. For example, how are you defining "good girl"? Is your anxiety always bad? What do you mean by "nicer"?

Notice that the judgments about yourself *(I did a terrible job)* and other people *(He's an idiot)* depend on perspective and who's doing the thinking—in this case, you! When we let our mind's judgments guide our behavior, we might lose sight of the bigger picture and miss out on experiences we value.

ACT Daily Writing: Judgments Vs. Observations

Write down positive and negative self-judgments. For example, *I'm friendly* and *I'm too short*.

_____
_____
_____

Now write your self-judgments as observations. Include observable facts or words that give context and perspective, such as "sometimes" and "in my/their opinion." For example, *Sometimes I make time to chat* and *I'm five-foot-three.*

_____
_____

What differences do you notice between self-judgments and observations?

_____
_____
_____
_____

Try It Now: Unhook From Judgments

Another helpful practice is to not take your judgments so seriously. Notice judgments as language that hooks you and try to unhook from them by seeing them as just words. Write down a self-judgment you struggle with (e.g., *I am fat*):

_____

Now write that judgment over and over in different ways: with your nondominant hand, backward, in cursive, tiny, big (e.g., FAT, taf, *fat*...).

_____

_____

What happened to the judgment?

_____

ACT in My Life: Today's Values, Goals, Reflections

_____
_____
_____
_____
_____
_____
_____
_____

Today's Practice

Notice your judgments (good and bad) today. When you notice them, try either restating them as observations or seeing them as just words. Write the judgments down and play around with them. See how this changes your perspective.

Date: _____

Day 5: Rules and Being Right

Diana: *When it comes to work, I'm a rule follower. I was the kind of kid who didn't have to be told to do my homework and the kind of graduate student who stayed in the lab instead of heading to happy hour. Although these rules helped me reach career goals, they also blocked me from other important things—like making time for friends. I haven't outgrown my work "rules," but my response to them has changed. Sometimes that means following my mind's "rules," but not always. Yesterday I woke early to write more of this book, but today I chose to make pancakes with my kids instead. I now notice my "rules," use them flexibly, and take actions that line up with the life I want to build.*

Our mind loves to follow rules. Rules can be helpful for organizing behavior and solving problems. For instance, the rule to wear your seatbelt has kept you safe. However, when you rigidly follow your mind's rules, you prevent adaptation and values-based action. Sometimes you must let go of rules to flexibly respond to life's circumstances.

Our mind also wants others to follow our rules, and we can latch on to being right. When this happens, we lose sight of what's really important. As therapists, we've both seen marriages destroyed over partners believing too firmly they were right. What happens when you're fixated on being right, but others disagree? Or when being right makes you chronically frustrated with the world or disappointed in people you care about?

ACT Daily Writing: Your Rules

We may not notice our mind's rules and righteousness, even if they limit us. For example, here are a couple of our rules: *If I say no to my friends, I'll hurt their feelings,* and *I can't feed my kids processed food because it's unhealthy.*

Write some of your rules.

What does your mind tell you "you're right" about but not everyone agrees? How are rule following and being right limiting you?

_____
_____
_____

Try It Now: Unconscious Rules

Notice some rules you're following *right now* that you're not usually conscious of. How many can you count? Are you wearing matching socks? Drinking your coffee from a mug and not a bowl? Wearing shoes outside? Sitting in a chair and not on the floor?

_____
_____
_____

Now consider whether some of these rules are less or more helpful to you? What would it be like to experiment with breaking some of these rules, just for the sake of practicing flexibility?

_____
_____

ACT in My Life: Today's Values, Goals, Reflections

_____
_____
_____
_____
_____
_____
_____
_____
_____

Today's Practice

Today, pick out a rule that you want to be less trapped by. Make a commitment to break that rule today. See what happens if you rebel against your mind!

Date: _____

Day 6: Comparisons and Shoulds

One of the wondrous things about the human mind is its ability to think abstractly. We can think of new ideas and create things that don't exist. We can compare ourselves to others and think about how we'd like things to be different.

Debbie: *I have a hand-me-down couch in my living room. It's slouchy and shows evidence that my kids love coloring on the couch. I feel embarrassed by it, and every time I visit a friend with a knack for home design, I can't help but compare: I should have nicer furniture by now! The thing is, when I think this way, my mind leaves out some other important information: I'm so lucky that I have a safe and comfortable place to live. I feel good about the environmental impact of reusing items. My couch is pretty comfortable, and I don't have to worry when my kids spill beverages on* *it. When my mind's caught up in comparing, I lose sight of what I have.*

The dark side of comparing ourselves to others is that we can create high standards and come up with all kinds of *shoulds*—ideas about what we should (or should not) be doing. We can dream up an ideal world in which we never measure up. Here are some of our unhelpful shoulds:

- *My partner should appreciate that I swept the floor.*
- *I should respond to an email the same day I receive it.*
- *I shouldn't have people over until my house is perfectly clean.*
- *My friends should know it's my birthday and call me.*

ACT Daily Writing: Noticing Shoulds

Write down some of the shoulds that might be limiting you (e.g., I should..., I shouldn't..., they should..., they shouldn't...).

_____

_____

How are these shoulds preventing you from doing what you care about? If you didn't follow them, how could your life be different? What would it be like to loosen up on those standards and to be more flexible with yourself?

_____
_____
_____

ACT in My Life: Today's Values, Goals, Reflections

_____
_____
_____
_____

Today's Practice

Pay special attention to how your shoulds, and other comparisons, are showing up for you today. Try doing things differently. When comparisons show up, keep your eyes on your own plate ... and how full it is! Try challenging a should today. Experiment by not doing it and doing something you *want* to do instead.

Date: _____

Day 7: Watering Seeds

Diana: *On a meditation retreat with Thich Nhat Hanh I learned about the mind training of "watering seeds." Put simply, our thoughts are like seeds in the garden of our mind. Some seeds will grow into plants we hope to harvest from someday. Other seeds will grow into weeds that can take over a garden bed. It's up to us to choose which seeds we want to water with our attention and our actions. Modern neuroscience supports these ancient teachings. When we defuse from unhelpful thoughts and act on our values instead, we shape neural connections and our behavior (Hanson 2020a). We can use our actions to water the person we want to grow.*

Sometimes we want to take action, but our mind gives us terrible advice—You can't do that; you aren't good enough. Just do it later, and why bother anyway?—stalling us with doubt or procrastination. This "advice" is intended to protect us; our mind judges and criticizes to shield us from things that could be physically or socially dangerous. But our mind can go too far when unhelpful thoughts keep us from doing things that are important to us. As Tara Mohr (2014) describes in her book *Playing Big*, when we listen to our inner critic—which guides us to *avoid* pain—we hide, don't speak up, and shy away from our truest callings.

Instead of giving attention to your mind's unhelpful advice, you can water seeds in your mind that encourage what Mohr calls "taking a leap" toward what matters most.

ACT Daily Writing: Mind Watering

Let's see how mind watering can help you take a leap. Write down one thing that you want to do but can't seem to muster the courage to do (e.g., start a blog or an exercise program, take on a new work responsibility).

What unhelpful advice has your mind given when it comes to "playing big" in this area? What unhelpful thoughts would you like to lay fallow?

_____

_____

What more helpful thoughts would you like to water with your attention?

_____

_____

Think back to a time when you did something you didn't think you could do or didn't want to do. What did this experience tell you about who's in charge of the garden of your life?

_____

_____

ACT in My Life: Today's Values, Goals, Reflections

_____
_____
_____
_____

Today's Practice

Tend to your inner garden today. Notice which seeds you're watering. If an unhelpful thought arises, simply let it pass—let it go fallow, as you would a weed. And notice the thoughts that are aligned with your values. Water those thoughts with your attention and actions.

Final Reflections

This week you worked on looking at your thoughts in a new way. You learned that you have an inner chatterbox, and that you don't have to take your thoughts so seriously. You learned to step back and defuse from your thoughts and water the ones that are most useful to you. What lessons would you like to remember? Your mind will most likely have a lot to say as you continue your work in *ACT Daily*. When you get hooked by its unhelpful commentary, don't forget that you can always *defuse* from your thoughts!

Week 4
Acceptance—Courageous, Willing, and Open

Diana: *My husband drives a 2001 Subaru with a peeling problem. I hate the car. When I park next to it in the driveway I comment internally,* Ugh, that car. *Even imagining it now makes me irritable. Meanwhile, my husband happily drives his old clunker around town, not obsessing about the peeling paint on the hood. He doesn't like the car either yet accepts these feelings so that he can focus on other things that are important to him—such as the students he works with. As for me, the more I focus my energy on wishing things were different, the more my suffering grows.*

Resisting and rejecting our inner experiences causes much of our psychological suffering. There is a reason why ACT is called *acceptance* and commitment therapy. Acceptance is a key process in psychological health (Forsyth and Ritzert 2018).

When we stop struggling with our experience, we free ourselves up to make choices that are consistent with our values. It's like dropping the rope in a tug-of-war with yourself so that you can use your hands for things that matter to you. Psychological acceptance does not mean that you have to "like" or "approve" of what life is offering. Acceptance means opening up to your moment-to-moment experience with receptivity, flexibility, and nonjudgment (Hayes, Strosahl, and Wilson 2012).

Acceptance sounds good when we experience emotions we like (such as joy, contentment, pleasure), but when we have more painful emotions (such as sadness, fear, or anger) we often reject, avoid, or suppress the feelings that come with them. When trying to get rid of difficult inner experiences means turning away from what matters to you, you engage in what is called experiential avoidance, *which is the opposite of acceptance.*

We all do things to move away from what we don't like, and that's neither bad nor good. But, it's helpful to notice when we are caught in a harmful circle of avoidance.

The Experiential Avoidance Roundabout

It's normal to not want to experience discomfort. To keep you safe, your brain evolved to problem solve ways for you to escape and avoid pain. If it's cold outside, you find shelter. If a car swerves at you, you try to dodge it. Attempts to avoid and control pain keep you safe from *physical harm,* but this strategy backfires when you use it with *psychological pain.* Why? Avoiding psychological pain:
- Is a short-term solution, and what you're avoiding will return
- Can intensify the very experiences you're trying to suppress
- Consumes resources that you could be using for other things that matter to you
- Restricts positive emotions
- Introduces a whole new set of problems

- Loops us in a cycle of psychological suffering

Experiential avoidance sends us around and around the roundabout of suffering. When we keep turning away from discomfort, we can end up in what Kevin Polk and colleagues (2016) call "stuck loops." These loops of experiential avoidance contribute to the development and maintenance of many of our mental health problems (Chawla and Ostafin 2007). Notice in the following examples how nonacceptance not only keeps one stuck but also blocks the opportunity for growth:

- You feel anxious about a work assignment, so you procrastinate, only to be more anxious.
- You're critical about your body, so you don't buy new clothes, only to feel worse about how you look.
- You feel embarrassment, so you don't speak up in social settings, only to feel less confident.
- You feel guilty about your alcohol use, so you drink to make that feeling go away, only to feel more guilty in the morning.

The Path of Acceptance

Are you stuck in a roundabout with your feelings and behaviors? Want a way out of this pernicious cycle? Do you want to get your life moving toward your values, even when the discomfort of living shows up? *Acceptance is your path through.*

Rather than pushing away painful private experiences, you move toward them willingly. You open yourself to the possibility that there's freedom in accepting your full life experience. As you become more comfortable accepting aspects of your internal experience, good and bad, you might find that acceptance offers you gifts, such as peace, understanding, and deeper meaning.

Acceptance also benefits the people around you. Imagine how you would engage your friends, your family, or even yourself differently if you accepted your inner experiences more fully.

This week you'll uncover the costs of nonacceptance and practice a path forward—one that involves courage and willingness. We hope you also uncover the gifts of saying yes to your full life experience.

Date: _____

Day 1: "Just Be Happy"

When someone asks, "How are you?" do you sometimes say "good," even when you're not? How about when someone asks, "What do you want?" Do you sometimes say, "I don't care" when you really do? We are all born with strong feelings and wants, and we freely express them as babies. But over time most of us learn that some types of inner experiences should be controlled, should not be shown in public, or should be modified to meet others' expectations. Certain thoughts and emotions are considered undesirable, signs of weakness, or things to be suffered alone. We're given messages like "just be happy," "boys don't cry," "keep it together," and over time we learn to control or hide what's deemed unacceptable. Sadly, hiding or suppressing our feelings also often means we cover up what matters to us, including our very selves.

Debbie: *Like many girls, I learned that expressing anger wasn't okay.*

When tempers flared, I felt scared and unsure of how to respond. Even while training to become a psychologist, I felt uncomfortable whenever a client expressed rage in the therapy room. I was disconnected from feelings of anger and had trouble expressing anger in a healthy way. I'm still working on it, but now I can see how believing these messages about anger have kept me from openly feeling an emotion we all have. I'm learning to stay in the presence of anger and to express it myself when necessary.

You have a diversity of feelings and sensations "under your skin." Some you may like and want to keep around, others not so much. But, as opposed to society's messaging, we have much less ability to control these private inner events than we think.

The acronym TEAMS (Robinson, Gould, and Strosahl 2011) is a useful way to look at our inner experience:

>**T**houghts such as judgments, rules, plans, or worries
>
>**E**motions such as fear, excitement, love, or embarrassment

Action tendencies such as urges, longings, or cravings

Memories such as past events or interactions

Sensations such as physical pain, comfort, or pleasure

Let's explore the messages you've received about your TEAMS.

ACT Daily Writing: Your TEAMS

What did you learn about expressing your thoughts and feelings growing up? Which TEAMS were "acceptable" to show? Which weren't? How were these messages influenced by your culture of origin or other identities, such as gender, age, race, physical ability, or sexual orientation?

_____
_____
_____

Do these messages influence you now? How do you want to approach your difficult TEAMS?

ACT in My Life: Today's Values, Goals, Reflections

_____
_____
_____
_____
_____
_____
_____
_____
_____
_____
_____
_____

Today's Practice

Pay more attention to what's happening "under your skin." Check in often and notice what TEAMS you're experiencing. Notice times you experience an inner state you don't want, and how you try to get rid of it. What would happen if you did something different?

Date: _____

Day 2: Experiential Avoidance Roundabouts

Diana: *People are really more similar than different. Whether I'm working with a teenager who binge eats or a dad who binge drinks, underneath is a desire to avoid the unease of living. I get it. I have my own avoidance strategies. ACT helps us spot our tendencies to avoid and then gently redirect ourselves toward our common longing to live well.*

We all numb out, distract ourselves, or check out of life sometimes. Do you grab your phone when you're bored? Snack when stressed? Online shop when you're down? Nir Eyal (2019) argues that a primary reason technology is so captivating is that it helps us avoid life's discomfort.

Experiential avoidance strategies aren't always harmful. But problems can arise when they pull you away from valued living. It's fine to pull out your phone while waiting in line, but spending hours on it every day, or checking email while in a heartfelt conversation with a good friend, could definitely be a problem.

If you're aware of your common avoidance strategies, you can recognize when they're destructive and keeping you in stuck loops. Circle the experiential avoidance strategies you use frequently (adapted and expanded from Harris 2019):

- **Numbing:** Do you overeat, restrict food, drink, use substances, overexercise, or harm yourself?
- **Bracing your body:** Do you tense up, clench your jaw, tighten your belly, or hold your breath?
- **Distracting:** Do you fantasize, think about something else, make jokes, thrill seek, multitask, or overuse technology?
- **Giving up:** Do you avoid signing up, isolate, sleep too much, say no, cancel, or hide?
- **Rushing through:** Do you overwork, stay constantly busy, strive for more, talk quickly, or move quickly through life?

- **Overthinking:** Do you intellectualize, ruminate, worry, mentally problem solve, or overanalyze?
- **Blaming:** Do you point fingers, judge, or criticize yourself or others?

ACT Daily Writing: Your Experiential Avoidance Patterns

Explore the avoidance strategies you circled above. Do they help you? Do they ever cause you to miss out on anything important? Are there short-term benefits? What about long-term costs?

_____
_____
_____
_____
_____
_____
_____

Try It Now: Name Your Roundabout

Try this strategy (Polk et al. 2016) to unhook from your stuck loops. Pick one of the avoidance strategies from the list above that causes you the most harm. What would you name it? Now say out loud: This is [your name], in an avoidance roundabout called _____.

Here are a couple of examples:

This is Diana in an avoidance roundabout of overscheduling.

This is Debbie in an avoidance roundabout of distracting with my phone.

Say yours a few times. What happens?

ACT in My Life: Today's Values, Goals, Reflections

Today's Practice

Be on the lookout for ways you avoid difficult thoughts and emotions. When you spot an experiential avoidance roundabout, think about the short- and long-term consequences. Name your experiential avoidance roundabout out loud, and ask yourself if there's another direction you'd like to head instead.

Date: _____

Day 3: The Fixing Trap

Diana: *When I'm stressed, I go through my day seeing everything that's wrong. I'm behind on paperwork, my clothes are out of date, my dog jumps on people. The more I focus on problems, the more problems I see, especially in myself. So, I try to "fix" my irritation by rushing around, nagging my family, myself, even my dog. There is a cost to this "fixing"—I miss out on seeing the good that sits alongside my messy life.*

Often when things aren't the way we want them to be we immediately try and fix them. We turn to our "righting reflex"—that is, our "built-in desire to set things right" (Miller and Rollnick 2012)—to fix the uncomfortable feeling that things aren't quite right.

Do you turn to fixing or self-improvement as a solution when faced with discomfort? Do you tell yourself that if you just got in shape, painted the walls, worked harder, or bought something new, then you'd finally feel better? It sounds good and healthy to try the latest self-help program, strive for spiritual enlightenment, go to therapy, or try a new diet or exercise program. As Pema Chödrön (2001) notes in *The Wisdom of No Escape and the Path of Loving-Kindness,* sometimes trying to change yourself can be a form of self-aggression. There's a dark side when self-improvement becomes *fixing* yourself, as though there's something fundamentally wrong with you. When you believe this, the very doubts and insecurities that spurred you to change grow stronger, and your dissatisfaction with yourself amplifies.

ACT Daily Writing: Your Fixing Trap

What are some of the qualities you try to "fix" about yourself? What do you do to try to improve yourself? Are there times when trying to fix yourself doesn't help?

Instead of rejecting yourself as not being good enough as you are, what else could you do?

Try It Now: Spotting Sunsets

Think of something in your life that you've been trying to fix or solve, such as your body, your anxiety, or your negative thoughts. What if this is not a problem to solve? Try looking at this inner experience as if it were a sunset—something to be observed and enjoyed—rather than a math problem to be solved (Wilson and DuFrene 2009). What can you appreciate about your experience? How is it beautiful in its own right?

ACT in My Life: Today's Values, Goals, Reflections

_____
_____
_____
_____
_____
_____
_____
_____
_____
_____
_____
_____

Today's Practice

Notice your tendency to get caught in the *fixing trap*—an urge to fix inner feelings about yourself and the environment around you. What does it feel like to engage in fixing? What happens when you drop the idea of setting things right?

Date: _____

Day 4: Willingness

If we want to stop trying to control, avoid, or fix our experience, what can we do instead? Develop willingness! In ACT, *willingness* is the courage to experience our unpleasant TEAMS in order to do the things that matter to us (Hayes, Strosahl, and Wilson 2012). You practice willingness every time you move outside your comfort zone.

Debbie: *I enjoy swimming laps, but I hate the sensation of getting into the pool. The water is chilly, and the first minute feels like shock. I'll spend hours dreading that one minute, mentally debating whether it's worth it. Sometimes I want to avoid that sensation so much that I go for a walk instead, or even skip exercising altogether. If I want to enjoy a swim, I have to be willing to feel the shock of cold water. When I do, it only lasts a minute, and then for the rest of the day I get to enjoy the benefits of swimming.*

As ACT therapists, we often feel like "willingness personal trainers." We help our clients start small—*Are you willing to feel anxiety right now?*—and work our way up to higher-intensity moves—*Are you willing to feel anxiety while asking your boss for time off?* It's inspiring to see willingness in action. It takes courage to turn toward painful things and to step into uncertainty or discomfort.

You probably already know what willingness feels like:

- Have you attended a function where you didn't know anyone?
- Have you asked for what you need in a relationship?
- Have you gotten out of bed even when you didn't feel like it?
- Have you resisted a temptation or an urge?

These uncomfortable activities show that you can have your TEAMS and choose to engage anyway. Today you're going to strengthen your willingness muscles by deliberately stepping outside your comfort zone.

ACT Daily Writing: Your Comfort Zone

It takes courage, willingness, acceptance, and self-compassion to make a move outside your comfort zone. When have you stepped out of your comfort zone and what was the result?

_____

_____

In the circles below, write some actions that are inside and outside your comfort zone now.

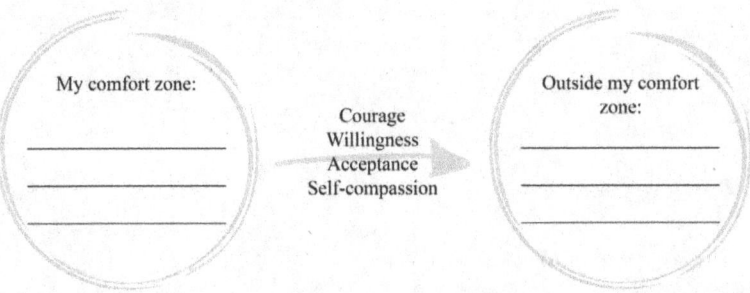

What do you miss out on when you stay in your comfort zone? What could you gain if you stepped outside it?

_____

_____

Try It Now: Make Room for Courage

Think about a courageous move you've wanted to make. Are you uncomfortable just thinking about it? Notice the discomfort inside your body. Imagine yourself as a soft, flexible container for these feelings. Instead of trying to squash or evict them, make room in your container—the bigger the discomfort the bigger the space. Imagine carrying these feelings with you as you step out with courage and self-compassion.

ACT in My Life: Today's Values, Goals, Reflections

_____
_____
_____
_____
_____
_____
_____
_____

Today's Practice

Flex your willingness muscles by choosing an uncomfortable task you've been avoiding—and take a step toward it. Choose something important that requires courage. Make space for the feelings that show up, and remind yourself you're doing willingness strength training!

Date: _____

Day 5: From Closing Off to Opening Up

Debbie: *One day in a parking lot I opened my car door too far and it lightly bumped the car next to me. No damage was done, but a man who saw my mistake made a rude comment. I immediately felt angry, and hours later I was still stewing. What a jerk! I kept trying to let the experience go, but it was all I could think about. At some point I realized that the real emotion I was feeling was embarrassment. I had made a careless mistake, and he saw me. When I turned toward my more vulnerable emotion of embarrassment I finally got unstuck.*

We can feel vulnerable when opening ourselves to the emotions we've been trained not to feel. If you've received the message that certain emotions are scary or even a sign of weakness, you might have learned to run away from them. Or maybe you turn your feelings outward, as Debbie did with the man in the parking lot, mistaking embarrassment for anger. That, too, is a form of avoiding emotions you think you shouldn't feel.

Despite what society may have taught you, there can be a lot to gain by turning toward your emotions and sensations. Your emotions serve a purpose; they can provide you with information about your needs and motivate you to make changes. Emotions such as anger, sadness, and guilt maintain our social fabric and connection. Imagine how difficult it would be to connect with a person who had no emotion.

Not accepting emotions has consequences. We punish ourselves for what we feel without even realizing it. We don't take risks. We live smaller, more painful lives. By opening up to and getting curious about our inner world, we can better use our experience to navigate our outer world effectively. Willingness and acceptance aren't just about purposely doing things that feel difficult; they also help us face our TEAMS when we are taking values-based actions.

ACT Daily Writing: Open Up

Write about something unpleasant you've been closing yourself off to or running away from. What do you miss out on when you close yourself off? What emotions would you likely feel if you were to move toward and open up to this situation instead?

_____
_____
_____
_____
_____

ACT in My Life: Today's Values, Goals, Reflections

_____
_____
_____
_____
_____

Today's Practice

Today notice your urge to close yourself off to unwanted inner experiences and situations. Instead practice gently opening yourself to them. You can open up with your:

Body—gently contact the uncomfortable feeling, and allow it with your body.

Mind—imagine yourself saying yes to what is.

Behavior—take an action that moves you toward what you care about even if it's uncomfortable.

The more you practice opening up, the more freedom you will experience.

Date: _____

Day 6: Sea Creatures and Pain—Hold Them Lightly

Diana: *Sometimes I'll ask teenage clients, "Are you a sea urchin or a sea anemone?" After their eye roll, I continue: "You see, sea urchins protect their tender insides with sharp spines. Sea anemones wear their tenderness on their skin and close up when threatened. It helps me to know because it's best to hold sea urchins lightly and approach sea anemones with gentleness."*

Are you a sea urchin or sea anemone? Do you get prickly or close up when you're feeling pain? We all defend ourselves against discomfort. You may have even noticed this this week as you've been working on acceptance. Just like engaging in therapy with a prickly teenager, maybe it would be more effective to approach your tender spots more gently and hold them lightly. Holding your pain lightly changes your experience of it:

- Letting go of muscle tension can change the quality of physical pain.
- Gingerly exploring memories of a trauma facilitates healing.
- Bringing humor to your vulnerabilities can help you take yourself less seriously.
- Sharing a painful experience with another lightens the load.

Today we'll work on ways you can hold your discomfort more lightly.

ACT Daily Writing: Loosen Your Grip

What kind of sea creature are you? Do you tend to prickle in response to pain, or shrink away from it? What would you like to do instead? Would it help to loosen your grip, bring a little humor to it, or connect with someone?

_____
_____
_____
_____
_____

Looking at the day ahead, what do you anticipate will be hard? Is there something you're likely to resist, brace against, or close off to? How could you hold your inner experience more gingerly in this area?

_____
_____
_____

Try It Now: Holding Pain

Cup your hands. Imagine that inside them you hold something—a relationship, a physical pain, a difficult situation—that is painful to you right now. Close your eyes and imagine yourself holding it like you would a delicate sea creature. Take three breaths as you hold your pain lightly and with care.

ACT in My Life: Today's Values, Goals, Reflections

_____
_____
_____
_____
_____
_____
_____
_____
_____
_____
_____

Today's Practice

Today notice when you're getting prickly or closing up in the face of discomfort. Pay attention to yourself locking your jaw, holding your breath, or tightening your shoulders. When you notice yourself resisting with your body, take a deep breath and loosen your grip a bit. Recommit to holding your experience lightly in your heart and body.

Date: _____

Day 7: Values and Pain Joined at the Hip

This week you've been brave. You've looked deeply at your experiential avoidance roundabouts and tried a new approach: acceptance. You've worked on your willingness to stop fixing, on stepping outside your comfort zone, and on holding your pain with care. By cultivating acceptance you've given yourself a beautiful gift. By being willing to accept pain, you've freed yourself to pursue what really matters to you. Pain and values are joined at the hip; you can't have one without the other. As Steven Hayes writes, "You hurt where you care, and you care where you hurt" (2019, 24).

Debbie: *No experience has been more challenging to me than parenting. I sacrificed many of life's pleasures for my children, such as lingering in bed with coffee and a good book on Saturday mornings. I've never cried more than when my newborn daughter* *was in the hospital. I've felt impatient with my kids, bored by tedious children's board games, and exhausted from sleep deprivation. I worry about parenting decisions, and whether I'm messing up. I'd love not to feel any of that, but would I give this experience up? Of course not. I love them deeply, and my pain is a consequence of caring so much.*

Think about something you care about deeply. Do you notice that it also comes with pain? What about something that is painful for you? Is there something you care about hidden underneath? If you didn't care, it wouldn't hurt as much. Acceptance gives you the flexibility to pursue what and who is most important to you, even when the pain of caring shows up.

Choosing to live your values means choosing to have pain.

As the Dalai Lama and Desmond Tutu have said, "Nothing beautiful comes without some suffering" (Dalai Lama, Tutu, and Abrahams 2016, 43). What beautiful things might happen in your own life if you're willing to care?

Daily ACT Writing: Exploring Values and Pain

Note a time in your life when you experienced pain and hardship. What did that experience tell you about what is most important to you?

_____
_____

What in your life is painful for you today? What does the pain say about what is important to you right now?

_____
_____

ACT in My Life: Today's Values, Goals, Reflections

_____
_____
_____
_____
_____
_____
_____

Today's Practice

Consider an area of your life that you care about but have been avoiding in some way. For instance, avoiding caring for your health, procrastinating on work, or distancing yourself from someone you care about. Remind yourself that it's uncomfortable because you care. Identify what you care about in this area and use values as a motivator to take a small step toward meaningful action today.

Final Reflections

This week you learned about some of the ways you might have avoided or tried to fix aspects of your experience. You practiced courage, willingness, openness, and acceptance as an alternative to experiential avoidance. You looked to your discomfort to learn about your deeply held values. All this will be helpful as you move on to the weeks ahead, in which you'll unhook from the stories you tell yourself and take action where it matters most to you.

Week 5

Perspective Taking—Take In the View

Diana: *Summer mornings can get fogged in here in coastal Santa Barbara. Locals call it "gray May," "June gloom," and "August fogust." Tourists who pay lots of money for oceanfront views crawl back into bed disappointed when they wake up to drizzle. Meanwhile, locals are busy packing their beach bags and putting sunscreen on their kids. What locals know is that fog is temporary, and by most afternoons it will have burned off to reveal big clear skies.*

Our mind can be a bit like a tourist who's new to an area and doesn't know what to expect there. The fog of predetermined beliefs about ourselves and the world filters our experience and blocks a bigger view. We humans construct stories to understand the world and find our way of belonging in it. But when our stories are inflexible, or we can't see past them, they skew our experience. We defend our self-image at the cost of real connection with others or build up our self-esteem at the cost of falling hard when we're deemed "average" (Neff 2015). Humans yearn for connection and belonging (Hayes 2019), and our conceptualized self-stories prevent us from learning, experiencing intimacy, and seeing our part in a greater whole.

Have you been caught in a self-story? Check any of the following scenarios that apply to you:

☐ Have you believed the story that you aren't "good" at something, so you didn't even try?

☐ Have you believed the story that you're "really good" at something, so you were self-critical when it became challenging?

☐ Have you been so stuck in making a good impression that you didn't hear the person you're with?

☐ Have you been boxed in by a story and missed other factors contributing to your experience?

There are often consequences of being boxed in by self-stories:
- You miss out on the here and now.
- You don't see how context is influencing your behavior.
- You're inflexible in your behaviors and beliefs.
- You seek out evidence to confirm what you already know.
- You lack the ability to take others' perspectives and offer empathy.
- You create self-fulfilling prophecies and miss opportunities to learn and grow.
- You feel disconnected from a greater whole.

You are more than the stories your mind creates. All of your inner experiences, including your self-stories, are phenomena that arise in the field of your attention and, eventually, pass, just like the weather. There's a version of you that can hold these experiences like the sky holds a passing weather system.

We want to direct your attention to the sky *itself*. The sky is a *transcendent you:* not your story of who you are, but the version of you who observes all the thoughts, emotions, and stories you have. This transcendent you was behind your eyes at age five and will be behind those same eyes at ninety-five. You will have many experiences in life, but you cannot be completely defined by any one of them; there is a version of you who transcends them.

This week you'll use perspective-taking skills to make contact with this transcendent version of you. You'll identify your self-stories and observe your experience from a new point of view. You'll move beyond defining yourself by the content of your story to having a more holistic view of yourself as someone shaped by the context of your learning history and the world around you. Doing this will help you respond more flexibly to life's challenges, see your experience with greater clarity, connect more deeply with others, and imagine new possibilities for yourself. Sound good? Let's get started!

Date: _____

Day 1: I Am, I Can't, I Always...

Humans are prone to creating self-narratives. These narratives provide a coherent sense of self. They help us communicate to others and understand our place in the world (Villatte, Villatte, and Hayes 2016). But our verbal, storytelling brains can cause us problems when we they box us in. Look at these examples:
- I am intelligent.
- I never lie.
- I can't handle stress.
- I am an extrovert.
- I am an anxious person.
- I am the type of person who...

Notice a pattern? Phrases such as "I am," "I never," and "I can't" are clues that you're boxed in by a self-story. Instead of seeing that who you are is shaped by the context you're in (self-as-context), you've overidentified with the content of who and what you are (self-as-content; Hayes, Strosahl, and Wilson 2012). In reality, we are more nuanced than the stories we tell ourselves (McHugh, Stewart, and Almada 2019), but sometimes we forget this and get trapped by them—even by the positive ones.

Debbie: *I've been told I'm friendly. I like my* I'm friendly *self-story because I value being kind. But the truth is, I'm more complicated than that; sometimes I'm not friendly. And sometimes this story can box me in. When I'm caught in my* I'm friendly *story, I tend to want to please others, and I struggle to set limits with everyone from close friends to salespeople.*

By becoming aware of self-stories, you can notice how your actions are constrained by them. Welcoming a broader perspective gives you the room to choose your actions, rather than your stories choosing for you.

ACT Daily Writing: Putting Yourself in a Box

Using the self-story stems below, write down some of the beliefs you have about yourself.

I am _____.

I never _____.

I always _____.

I don't _____.

I can't _____.

Now, take a closer look. Are these stories *always* true of you, or are you more complicated than that?

Pick a statement from your list above. Give an example of a time this story was true for you and a time it wasn't.

_____
_____
_____

What situations or contexts trigger this story?

_____
_____

How do you act when it shows up? How does this story limit you? Does it prevent you from connecting with others or taking valued action?

_____
_____

Rewrite this story to include more context, nuance, and flexibility.

_____
_____
_____

ACT in My Life: Today's Values, Goals, Reflections

_____
_____
_____
_____
_____
_____
_____

Today's Practice

Catch yourself telling self-stories. Be on the lookout for clues that you're boxed in, such as "I am," "I always," "I never," and then step back and take a broader view.

Date: _____

Day 2: Meet Your Story

Our minds aren't always objective. As a politician's press secretary can bend "facts" to tell a particular story, our minds can take in information from the environment and alter it based on past experiences and predetermined beliefs. This self-story filter can interfere with our ability to see our present experience clearly. It can be helpful, instead, to develop skills that help us remove the storytelling filter and see things with greater clarity.

Diana: *Sometimes I play a game with my clients. I have them write down the day's problem on a note card but don't let them tell me what it is. Then I interview them about the story they have about the problem. "What story does your mind tell you about this problem? How long has this story been around? What percentage of the day are you entangled in it? If your best friend had the same story, what would you say to this person? What if a child you love had that story?" After the* *interview I ask them to reveal the problem.* I find that we can get a lot done in therapy when we step back from stories, and the same is true of getting things done in life.

A first step toward a more flexible view of yourself is to pay attention to your direct experience as it is, instead of through the self-story filter. Much like Diana does with her clients, you can use the skills you learned for being present in Week 2 to observe the story somewhat objectively. As ACT expert Dr. Rhonda Merwin (2020) shared on episode 128 of our podcast, you can "have your narrative without your narratives having you." Observing your inner narrative gives you a little wiggle room to help you get unstuck from even your stickiest self-stories.

ACT Daily Writing: Interview Your Self-Story

Distill in one to two sentences a self-story you're struggling with.

Now, interview yourself about the story. How long has it been around? What percentage of the day are you entangled in it? What would you say to a best friend or a child you love who has the same story?

_____
_____
_____
_____
_____
_____
_____

Try It Now: Just the Facts

Take the story you listed above and try describing and labeling it as a problem without a story attached. Out loud, finish these prompts and describe your problem with just the facts: "I am feeling...," "I am thinking...," "I am experiencing..." You can have your story without your story having you!

ACT in My Life: Today's Values, Goals, Reflections

_____
_____
_____
_____
_____
_____
_____
_____
_____
_____
_____
_____

Today's Practice

Notice when you're caught in a problem, big or small. Step back and identify a self-story linked to it. Try observing and describing your experience (your behavior, thoughts, emotions, sensations). Instead of using self-statements such as "I am," make observations like "I am feeling," "I am experiencing," or "I am thinking."

Date: _____

Day 3: Flexibility Training

Diana: *We don't have chairs or couches in front of screens in our home. We got rid of them to build in more "nutritious movement" (Bowman 2017). Without a predetermined place to sit, my family gets creative about what to do while watching a show or working. My boys toss a football while watching sports. I stretch my calves while editing podcasts. We've set up our home environment to build our physical flexibility.*

Just as having a flexible body makes you more resilient and better prepared to respond to life's obstacles, so, too, does having a flexible mind. Resilience is not about avoiding bad things, but about how you respond to them. By learning to flexibly shift out of the stories that box you in, you'll be better able to respond to life's challenges.

Self-stories can limit your range of effective responses—especially if your stories about yourself aren't consistent with the person you want to be. This may seem obvious with harsh or critical self-stories, such as *I'm unlovable.* If you believe that to be true of yourself, you might not go out on dates—a prerequisite to meeting a romantic partner. But it's also true with seemingly positive self-stories. For example, research shows that kids who are told they are smart are more likely to give up when problems are challenging (Dweck 2016).

You just might be surprised by what you can do when you look beyond what you believe to be true about yourself.

ACT Daily Writing: Mind Stretching

What story are you caught in right now? How is it limiting your range of motion? How can you stretch your mind a bit? What are some more flexible moves you could make?

_____
_____
_____
_____
_____

ACT in My Life: Today's Values, Goals, Reflections

_____
_____
_____
_____
_____
_____

Today's Practice

Choose a self-story that's been around a while. Today practice flexibility by deliberately doing the opposite of what the story says. If you tell yourself you're shy, talk to someone new. If you fancy yourself a night owl, go to bed early. If you tend to be a tidy person, leave some dirty dishes in the sink all day. Prove to the world that you are a complex person! Notice how this changes your perspective about yourself.

Date: _____

Day 4: Finding Sky Mind

Colorado is known for its big, clear skies, but on even the sunniest of June days afternoon thunderstorms can dramatically roll in, drenching hikers. Our mind is a lot like these Colorado skies. One moment our mind is big and clear, and the next it's stormy with self-stories. Just like the weather, no matter how bad or good our mind state is, it won't last forever. And, no matter how loud the thunder of our thoughts and emotions, it can't harm the sky.

Remember, behind every weather system there's always a big sky that remains unchanged.

Today you're going to step into a broader mind state, one we call "sky mind." Sky mind is the ability to open to all of your inner experiences, even the stormy ones. Sky mind doesn't shame anxiety thunderstorms or attach to happy rainbows but makes room for every system that passes. When you're using sky mind you have a grander perspective and feel more connected to people and the world around you. You may have experienced sky mind when hiking to the top of a mountain, engaging in spiritual practice, caring for a loved one, or being part of a group.

Your brain is constantly shifting between self-focus and a broader perspective, and there are evolutionary benefits to both (Hanson 2020a). But our modern Western culture overstimulates our self-focus. That's one reason why it's beneficial to deliberately practice shifting into sky mind. When you're in this mind state, you observe the panorama of your experience, rather than being caught up in the content of your daily life. This fosters cooperation, flexibility, and the feeling that you're part of a larger whole.

ACT Daily Writing: Your Sky Mind

Write about a time you experienced sky mind. What helps you find it? Where in your life would sky mind be helpful?

_____
_____
_____
_____
_____
_____

Try It Now: A New Horizon

According to neuropsychologist Rick Hanson, when your eyes are focused on close objects, more self-focused *egocentric* brain areas are activated (2020a). But when you look at the sky or the horizon, your brain shifts to an *allocentric* perspective, one that moves beyond you to seeing yourself as part of a bigger whole. Let's try this form of perspective taking:

1. Look at things that are close to you—the words of this book, your hands holding it.
2. Now, shift your eyes to the horizon or sky. Look out a window if you're inside. Follow a bird, or

look for a tree or a building far away.
3. What happens to your perspective?

ACT in My Life: Today's Values, Goals, Reflections

_____
_____
_____
_____
_____
_____

Today's Practice

Notice when you're caught up in the weather of a self-story. Move out of the content of what you're thinking and into the process of your experience. Look out at the horizon and see the bigger picture.

Date: _____

Day 5: Transcending Time

Think back over the past year. Remember all the ups and downs you experienced—how world events impacted you, your personal achievements and struggles, how you dealt with your daily problems. You had countless thoughts in your mind, emotions came and went, your body aged a year, and you took breath after breath. Through the year one thing remained constant—*you!* You were there, experiencing every bit of life along the way.

When we get caught up in our mind's chatter about ourselves and our current problems, we can lose track of our life over the course of time. It can help to zoom out one's perspective and see life as unfolding over time. Seeing a city from an airplane window can change our point of view, as does seeing the flow of our experience from a zoomed-out perspective. What looks like overwhelming chaos from the street looks quite different from ten thousand feet in the air. As Robyn Walser puts it, "As our consciousness stretches across time, we see change, we see the ongoing flow of life" (2019, 80).

One way to transcend time and to step into sky mind is to look at your own life from a zoomed-out perspective. We can feel both relief and sorrow when we recognize the subjective and impermanent nature of time. The best vacation will come to an end, and so will the pain of a sleepless night. And we are there to experience both, as well as all the ups and downs along the way.

ACT Daily Writing: Future Self, Past Self

Take a moment to zoom out on your life. Imagine visiting your five-year-old self. What would you like to say to this younger version of you? What would your younger self say to you now?

_____
_____
_____
_____

Now zoom out to your ninety-five-year-old self. What would your future self say to you now? What advice would your elder self give you?

_____
_____
_____
_____

Try It Now: Zoom Out

On this time line, imagine your life from birth to death. Take a guess where you are now and mark it with an *X*.

_____
Your Birth   Your Death

Think of all of the major events that have happened—your personal highs and lows that would zigzag up and down this line. Notice how your perspective changes when you look at your life from a broader vantage point.

ACT in My Life: Today's Values, Goals, Reflections

_____
_____
_____
_____
_____
_____
_____
_____
_____
_____
_____
_____
_____
_____

Today's Practice

Take this grander zoomed-out view as you go about your day today. How would a zoomed-out view change your sense of what matters most?

Date: _____

Day 6: Connect, Relate, and Belong

Debbie: *Over coffee with a friend, she shared with me about a painful problem. Without realizing it my mind drifted away, and I became preoccupied by my own worries about a similar problem and with mentally comparing myself to her. I was halfway tuning her out, caught in my own self-stories. When I realized this, I reoriented myself to focus on her struggle and to be the friend I want to be.*

At the heart of being human is the desire to relate, connect, and belong. The human brain is a social one, with areas devoted to social connection, perspective taking, and compassion. At times, when we're caught up in a self-story and our own ego, it can be hard to truly connect in relationships. Self-stories can fuel disconnection when you:

- Are preoccupied with comparing yourself to others

- Worry about fitting in and unintentionally push others away
- Interpret others' behavior through your own filters and assume the worst
- Don't take others' perspectives, making it difficult to have empathy and compassion

When you use sky mind, practice perspective taking, and step back from your own story you better connect with others. Perspective taking lies at the heart of conflict resolution, compassion, social justice, and authentic relationships. In *A Liberated Mind,* Steven Hayes writes, "As you emerge behind your eyes, you begin to see behind the eyes of others. You begin to find that you're making more thoughtful connections with people all the time … Empowering us to be more fully ourselves and yet deeply related to others" (2019, 176).

To show up fully in relationships and connect deeply, we must see past our own point of view to take in the richness of another's perspective.

ACT Daily Writing: Find Connection

Are there people you have trouble connecting with because you are caught in a self-story? What's another perspective you could take? How might you let go of this self-story and open up to more connection?

_____
_____
_____

ACT in My Life: Today's Values, Goals, Reflections

_____
_____
_____
_____
_____

Today's Practice

Choose a social interaction you will have today and commit to engaging it with sky mind. Step back from your self-story and get behind the other person's eyes and engage their worldview. Listen with every ounce of your being while they talk. Open up to them in a genuine way. Bring your focus back to the person every time your mind drifts away.

Notice how this type of connection feels different compared to times when a self-story pulled you away from relationships.

Date: _____

Day 7: Exploring Possibility

When you're stuck in a self-story, it can be hard to see all of life's possibilities. At times, you can get so focused on protecting your self-esteem, defending your self-stories, or achieving the outcome you want that you miss a chance to live out your dreams.

Debbie: *I have a holiday tradition of going to* The Nutcracker *ballet, and during the month of December I can be found twirling and leaping around my living room. One year, my husband watched my enthusiasm (and lack of skill) and said, "Maybe you should take a ballet class." A little seed of possibility was sparked.* Me? Ballet class? I haven't done that since I was nine years old! *My mind went through every self-story:* I'm too old, I don't have time, I'm not flexible enough. *But I couldn't shake the idea. Soon I found a small ballet studio that caters to beginner adults. Before I knew it, that seed of possibility had grown into something, and there I was at the barre, practicing pliés!*

Most of us can come up with plenty of reasons why trying something new won't work out. But what would it be like to explore the realm of possibility? Imagine taking a new perspective and thinking broadly about what life could be if you weren't bogged down by self-stories. What are you longing for? What do you dream about? What would be possible if you were free to choose what to do with no limitations? As Dr. Helen Neville (2020) notes on our podcast, "We should always be thinking about not what is logically possible, but what is impossible that we can make possible."

ACT Daily Writing: Exploring Possibility

Make a list of things you would secretly like to do. It's okay to note things that may never happen! We're working in the realm of possibility, not strictly in reality.

_____
_____
_____
_____
_____
_____

What does your list tell you about what you'd like to be doing? What are you longing for? What possibilities arise when you free yourself from the limits of reality?

_____
_____
_____
_____
_____

ACT in My Life: Today's Values, Goals, Reflections

_____
_____
_____
_____
_____
_____
_____
_____
_____
_____
_____
_____

Today's Practice

Today, step out of a self-story and live in the realm of possibility. You might even do one of the things on your list of things you'd secretly like to do. Whatever you do, however big or small, notice the magic that resides in possibility!

Final Reflections

Now that you've stepped back from your self-stories, found your sky mind, and discovered new possibilities, it's time to explore the directions you want to take your more flexible self! Take your new perspective with you as you move on to the rewarding task of exploring what and who matters most to you, and how you want to be in the world.

Week 6

Values—Choose Your Direction

A lot of self-help books will tell you how to change your life for the better and give you strategies for doing it. But we're not going to do that. Instead, we are going to make sure the changes you strive for are the ones you care deeply about.

What if instead of pursuing pleasure or unimportant goals, you focused on living your life in a way that provided a sense of meaning, purpose, and vitality? As Robyn Walser writes in *The Heart of ACT,* living according to our values "is deeper than daily activities that fill up our lives. It's deeper than a single goal or set of goals. It is about orienting our lives to a set of larger aspirations linked to creating personal meaning" (2019, 50).

Values are the glue that cements our daily actions to something greater than ourselves and our struggles. What does it mean for *you* to have a meaningful, fulfilling life? What type of friend, sibling, partner, community member, or worker do you want to be? If you had six months to live, what would matter most to you? These kinds of questions can guide our actions to take us toward a richer life. In our podcast, Jenna LeJeune (2019) comments that she's not interested in helping clients discover the meaning of life, rather she's interested in helping them discover what is meaningful for them. Our goal is the same in this journal.

Values

What exactly are values?
- They are about creating meaning, not seeking happiness.
- They provide a direction to guide you rather than being goals with end points.
- They are deeply personal and freely chosen by you and not based on expectations, predetermined moral standards, or social approval.

- They consist of qualities of action (e.g., forgiving) rather than domains in which you act (e.g., family).
- They won't guarantee a pain-free, pleasure-filled life.
- They are linked to vulnerability and won't prevent you from experiencing loss.

Even if we already know what's important to us, we might be waiting to act on it. We might think we need conditions to change, to feel "better," or for something about us to be "fixed" or improved before we can take important, values-driven steps. Here are some of our examples:

Diana: I'd like to play more with my kids, but I feel guilty about unfinished work.

Debbie: I want to write an article but am not confident enough to start.

Diana: I want to host more podcasts on what we can do about racism, but it can be so uncomfortable.

Debbie: I want to exercise more, but I'm waiting until I'm more motivated.

We can spend far too much time not doing the things we care about.

In ACT, you don't have to wait for anything to change in order to start living your values (Hayes, Strosahl, and Wilson 2012). There are always small, meaningful moves available to you, and you can start making them today.

This week you'll clarify your deeply held values and work toward bringing more of these qualities into your daily life. Much as an art curator would thoughtfully choose pieces to create an exhibit, you get to choose which values and values-based actions fit the kind of life you want to create—a life you can feel proud of, whatever your current circumstances.

Date: _____

Day 1: Pleasure or Meaning?

Debbie: *One day, feeling especially drained from work, I watched the people behind the counter at a bagel shop joke around and listen to music while making bagels. It looked fun! I imagined quitting my job as a psychologist and working there, where I imagined the emotional weight wouldn't be as heavy. I realized, though, that if I quit, I'd miss everything I love about my work.*

Most of us want to feel good. We might constantly seek pleasurable states, such as happiness and calm, hoping that someday they'll stick. But pleasurable feelings are fleeting. Engaging in activities just for the sake of pleasure may feel good for a while, but it doesn't lead to longer-term wellbeing (Huta and Ryan 2010). Over time, focusing narrowly on feeling good can lead one to feel adrift without purpose.

There's a more fulfilling path: the pursuit of a meaningful life. Think about your most impactful life experiences. Perhaps it was working hard for a degree, volunteering for a cause you care about, traveling, or even recovering from an injury or addiction. These experiences likely included some degree of stress or emotional pain, but in the long run living with meaning fosters a deeper form of satisfaction (Smith 2017) than seeking pleasure alone can. Meaningful engagement provides a sense that your actions matter. Even months later, people who engage in meaningful activities report having more positive moods, feeling more enriched, and having a sense of being a part of something greater (Huta and Ryan 2010). Having a sense of purpose in your life also predicts resilience in the face of adversity (Tedeschi and Calhoun 2004) and a longer life (Buettner 2008).

ACT Daily Writing: In Pursuit of Meaning

Jot down something that gives you pleasure but isn't that satisfying.

Now write about something you do that feels important or fulfilling, something that gives you a greater sense of purpose but isn't always enjoyable.

How is your experience different when you engage in what matters? Are there hard parts about engaging in this way?

How might you pursue meaning in your life now more often?

Try It Out: A Meaningful Moment

If you were to rewind your day yesterday and pause on a moment that stood out as rewarding to you, what would it be? What does this moment show you about what matters most in your life right now?

ACT in My Life: Today's Values, Goals, Reflections

_____
_____
_____
_____
_____
_____
_____
_____
_____
_____
_____
_____
_____
_____

Today's Practice

Do one small thing today that's bigger than yourself, that makes a difference in the world and feels worthwhile to you. It could be caring for someone else, taking an action that is good for the environment, or contributing to a cause that matters to you. Pay attention to how it feels to do this thing.

Date: _____

Day 2: Your Life Motto

In ACT, *values* are defined as qualities of *how* we live our life. We want to act in ways that feel consistent with the person we want to be in the world. When your actions aren't guided by your values, you can end up reacting to life's events randomly, with no consistent framework for how you would respond at your best.

Debbie: *You know how some emails have a quote or motto below the signature line? After feeling inspired by one I saw, I tried writing a little motto for myself. I thought about it a while and wrote: "Be Kind. Be Brave. Live Fully." To me, these words pretty much sum up how I want to live. This motto has stayed with me, and I think of these words when I need a reminder of my values.*

A good first step to pinpointing your personal values is to think about how you want to live and to clarify the qualities that matter to you. Here are just a few examples of the many qualities you might choose from:

Compassionate

Courageous

Curious

Fair

Funny

Generous

Hardworking

Humble

Independent

Kind

Loving

Loyal

Open

Responsible

Serious

To discover your own truest values, think about the most important qualities that you want to cultivate in your life. These are the qualities that would make you proud if others used them to describe you.

ACT Daily Writing: Qualities to Cultivate

Think of someone you admire—someone you know, or perhaps a famous or spiritual figure. What are the qualities you admire most about them?

_____
_____
_____
_____

Imagine that an important friend or family member was describing you to someone you'd never met. What qualities would you *most want* them to say about you?

Try It Now: Create Your Own Motto

If you were going to write a life motto for yourself, what would it be? What words or phrases would you be sure to include?

ACT in My Life: Today's Values, Goals, Reflections

_____
_____
_____
_____
_____
_____
_____
_____
_____
_____
_____
_____

Today's Practice

Think of one quality you'd most like to exhibit through your actions today. If you'll have trouble remembering it, write it down on a little piece of paper and carry it with you, or post it in a place where you'll see it frequently. As much as you can today, focus on bringing this quality out in small (and maybe big) ways in your actions and interactions with others.

Day 3: Values Where They Matter Most

Diana: *When Debbie and I decided to write a book together, I was secretly elated because it meant I'd get to spend more time with her. I tend to work alone, and I long to connect more often with close friends. By working on this journal together I engaged in my values of authentic friendship and doing impactful work that can improve people's lives. I call this taking "values-rich" actions, in which I can live out many values at once.*

When pinpointing values, people often say "I value my health" or "I value my family" and stop there. But what happens when you "value family" and choose to work late because you have a big deadline? Or maybe you value health but choose to eat cake to celebrate your friend's birthday? Are you giving up on your values? Of course not! Ultimately, important areas of your life, such as family, work, and community, are *domains* in which you *live out* your values in different ways, depending on the circumstances.

Sometimes it might feel like your values conflict. While it's true that you have to make choices about where you put your time and energy, this "conflict" is really an issue of prioritizing which value or quality to express in the moment. Your values usually overlap across multiple domains at any given moment, and you don't have to resolve domain conflicts, rather you can look to how they can enrich each other (Schonbrun 2014; Schonbrun and Corey 2020). Don't forget that you can also live out many values at once within each domain, as Diana does with her values-rich actions. It's not always easy, but we can find ways to show up with our values where it's important.

ACT Daily Writing: Revitalize with Values

Circle a few areas of your life that feel important to you right now, perhaps ones you've been neglecting:

Family

Romantic partner

Work or education

Community

Leisure

Physical self-care

Creative expression

Spirituality

Environment

Friendship

Personal growth

Other: _____

What do you care most about in these areas?

_____
_____
_____
_____

What actions could reflect your caring?

_____
_____
_____
_____
_____
_____

How could this caring spread to other life domains? How could you make your domains more values-rich?

_____
_____
_____
_____

ACT in My Life: Today's Values, Goals, Reflections

_____
_____
_____
_____
_____
_____
_____
_____

Today's Practice

Choose a domain of your life to reinvigorate. Bring more caring, creativity, and vitality to this domain by acting on your values. Notice what it feels like to engage in this way.

Date: _____

Day 4: A Place for Love to Go

Diana: *Santa Barbara is known for its beaches, but also its wildfires. When I was seven, I remember my mom packing up the car with our dog and bird and driving us through smoke to a friend's house to watch the fires on TV. In 2017 it was my turn as a mom to pack up my family and make our way through the smoke to safety. We gave each kid a shoebox to fill with his most special things. The chickens had to stay. Driving away I looked back at our house and knew that no matter what burned, my value of loving was coming with me.*

Have you had the experience of going about your life as usual and then everything changed quickly because of a big and unexpected life event, such as a job change, a natural disaster, war, a death or an illness, a car accident, or a pandemic? How did such an event change your perspective? Did it help you see what you love most in a new light?

Most of the time, values boil down to love.

You don't have to wait for an evacuation warning, a medical diagnosis, or losing a job to remind you of this. Instead you can take action every day as if love is the thing that really matters. Today you're going to explore the value of acting on love and create a few concrete reminders to add to your day.

ACT Daily Writing: What Would You Pack?

Imagine you had to evacuate your home quickly. What important items would you pack up? What do these objects show you about what you love most?

_____
_____
_____
_____

How could you act on that love today?

_____
_____
_____

ACT in My Life: Today's Values, Goals, Reflections

_____
_____
_____
_____
_____

Today's Practice

Values can be represented in words, pictures, objects, and sounds. Create something that depicts your values and will remind you to act from them. Here are some examples:

- A photo on your desktop

- A meaningful ringtone
- A note in your wallet
- A meaningful trinket or jewelry
- A sticker on your water bottle
- An email signature
- An object by your nightstand
- A really nice *ACT Daily* tattoo (we tried)

Be sure that this representation is something you'll engage with regularly.

Date: _____

Day 5: Choose a Direction

Values are often described as directions you can choose. No matter where you stand on the planet you can always point yourself north, south, east, or west, and no matter what's going on in your day, you can head toward a value. Goals, on the other hand, are the mountains, deserts, or rivers you cross along the way. Let's say you want to head in the direction of your "physical care" values, so you set a long-term goal of running a 10K and start training. But what if the race gets cancelled, or you get injured? Can you still point yourself in the direction of physical self-care? Of course! You may just need to adjust your goals.

Debbie: *I have had many clients who identify partnership or marriage as a goal and get discouraged when dating isn't going very well. I like to remind them of the deeper values, such as love, respect, and companionship, underlying their relationship goals and encourage them to live those values in* *every situation they can—with friends, at work, and on dates.*

You won't be able to live according to your values perfectly all the time. Sometimes you'll meet your goals, other times not, but you can always reorient yourself toward what you care about. We may aspire to reflect a quality we value *and* rarely feel like we are 100 percent where we want to be.

Go easy on yourself.

Part of the journey is reorienting, adapting, and carrying on. You've spent the last few days exploring directions you want to head. Today you'll identify some goals to help motivate you along the way. Next week you'll work on committed actions to achieve your goals.

ACT Daily Writing: Mountains to Climb

What are some important directions you want to head in your life? What are a few concrete goals you could reach along the way? Do you have a time line for reaching those goals?

Direction I want to head: _____
Goals along the way: _____

_____
_____
_____

Direction I want to head: _____
Goals along the way: _____

_____
_____
_____

Direction I want to head: _____
Goals along the way: _____

_____
_____
_____

ACT in My Life: Today's Values, Goals, Reflections

_____
_____
_____
_____
_____
_____
_____
_____
_____
_____
_____
_____

Today's Practice

Choose one of the directions you wrote about above and make a meaningful move (big or small) in that direction. Sign up for a race, call a friend, or get some art supplies. Take the first meaningful step in a direction that matters.

Date: _____

Day 6: Your Values Compass

Debbie: *Remember how my life motto includes the phrase "be kind"? Well, I have room for improvement, even regarding the people I love most. One day (okay, a lot of days) I was tired and irritable. My husband was trying to chat, but I was tuning him out, except to gripe at him. Later that night I felt guilty for having acted that way. I remembered that I want to be a kind and connected partner, even on my bad days. The next morning, I made sure to stop what I was doing, look straight at him, and "tune in."*

Sometimes in life we get off track. We all do. When that happens, tuning in to your values is like using a compass. A values compass helps you flexibly find your way no matter where you stand. With a values compass, you don't need to follow a premarked trail, so you have more freedom to venture into life's wilderness!

When you're setting your compass in the right direction, emotions and sensations can be guides, if you pay attention to them. Inner cues such as vitality, longing, regret, nostalgia, loss, or the pain of missing out can guide you. And when something "feels right" deep inside your body, it may indicate that you're headed in the right direction.

With your values compass set properly, you can stay on course and adapt to new terrain, navigating unexpected river crossings such as job changes, new relationships, conflicts, illness, loss, or relapse. In the end, it's not a question of *if* you'll stray from your values—we all do—but of what you do when you're off track.

ACT Daily Writing: Setting Your Compass

Write about a time when you were on track with your values. What did that feel like inside and out?

_____
_____
_____
_____

Now, thinking about your week so far, when have you acted in a way that felt off track from your values?

_____
_____
_____
_____

What does this tell you about how you might adjust course? How can you use ACT processes to adapt to unexpected obstacles? In what direction do you want to point your values compass in the week ahead?

ACT in My Life: Today's Values, Goals, Reflections

_____
_____
_____
_____
_____
_____
_____
_____
_____
_____
_____
_____

Today's Practice

Pay attention to inner cues today, such as sensations and emotions. Ask yourself what those cues teach you about how your life is going relative to your values. Notice if they point you in a direction you find fulfilling, and what it feels like when you're off course.

Date: _____

Day 7: Everything Will End

Diana: *There's a hugging meditation I learned while on a retreat with Thich Nhat Hanh (2003). He told us to hug someone we love with our whole being. Breathing in, we were reminded to remember that they are alive, and breathing out, to think about how good it feels to be alive together. On the next in-breath, we were to remember that we will grow old and die. Breathing out, we were to remember that our loved one, too, will grow old and die. While we hugged our loved one, we were told to breathe in the preciousness of this moment.*

Connecting with a sense of life's impermanence can reveal your deepest values. And, when you uncover your values, you cannot help but feel the inherent risk in living them. Living your values reveals the vulnerability of caring, the grief associated with change, and the certainty that everything will end. As Robyn Walser writes, "Awareness of death has the potential to instigate a radical shift in life perspective and motivate us to engage in being alive in the moment and commit to actions that serve our value" (2019, 75). Opening your heart wide to care deeply can feel terrifying; it requires touching unavoidable impermanence.

When you make intimate contact with your values, there's no going back to unknowing them. You feel their tug when making important decisions, their call when you stray from them, and their urgency when waking to your own mortality.

Today you'll explore how touching impermanence and vulnerability can help clarify what a well-lived life means for you.

ACT Daily Writing: Touching Impermanence

When you think about caring more deeply in your life, what vulnerabilities show up? What are you most afraid of losing? What are you most afraid of feeling?

What would it take to look back at your life, at the end, and feel satisfied that you'd lived well? What would give you a sense that you had lived fully?

Try It Now: A Year to Live

If you had a year to live, what would you most want to do?

What about a month to live? What would you do?

How about a day to live? What would it look like?

_____

What about an hour to live? What would you do with your last hour?

_____

And ... what if the next minute was your last?

_____

Choose some of the actions above and put them in your calendar—to be done over the following week, month, and year. Then take the next minute and do that most important thing.

ACT in My Life: Today's Values, Goals, Reflections

_____
_____
_____
_____
_____
_____
_____
_____

Today's Practice

Today, remember the impermanence of all things. Take an hour and live it as if it were your last. Use impermanence to guide your actions. Remind yourself of what a well-lived life would look like for you, and make a conscious choice to live well today.

Final Reflections

This week you clarified your values by looking at the qualities you would like to express in your life and the domains that matter most to you. You looked at areas of life where you might want to adjust course or set values-consistent goals. And you considered the big picture of what matters most to you when it's all said and done.

Anchor yourself in these values and carry them with you into your next ACT process.

Week 7

Committed Action—Fall on Purpose

Diana: *I've always been afraid of falling. As a kid I wouldn't climb trees and never made it past the bunny slopes skiing. In yoga I conveniently step out to use the bathroom when it's time for headstands. Then I learned that falling is part of committed action. In an ACT workshop, Kelly Wilson stood, wobbling in a yoga tree pose, and said, "What if falling were part of the pose?" Falling on purpose was radically freeing for me. If I fell on purpose it meant I could try all sorts of things! Surfing, a podcast, homeschooling, starting new friendships. Today committing to falling on purpose opens my life to fresh opportunities.*

It's human to have yearnings to grow, build mastery, and live in ways that matter (Hayes 2019). It's also human to be imperfect, fumble, and get derailed. As you've probably noticed in filling out this journal, progress is rarely linear. Some days you may read through the pages without writing anything, others you skip altogether, and yet for others you give 100 percent effort. Perfectly following the plan for a given day isn't what makes a difference in doing this journal, rather it's your action of picking it up, over and over again, and keeping at it. This is committed action.

Committed action involves three components (Moran, Bach, and Batten 2018):

1. **Taking action:** engaging in a behavior—not just thinking about it or talking about it, but acting on it
2. **Connecting to values:** acting in ways that are meaningful to you, personal, chosen by you, and intrinsically motivating
3. **Carrying on in the face of obstacles:** returning again to acting even when you stumble, are derailed by thoughts, or unsettled by urges and emotions

When people first learn about ACT, some think it means just accepting everything as it is and not changing anything. This is not true! In ACT, changing the things that aren't "working" in your life, and taking action to move toward what's most important to you, can be as important as acceptance.

This week you'll muster all of your psychological flexibility skills to create a compassionate, flexible committed action plan for yourself. Along the way you will:
- Explore your personal obstacles to change
- Use values to guide your actions
- Apply the science of behavior change to create contexts that support meaningful changes
- Practice flexibility with yourself

Are you ready? Sharpen your pencil and let's get to committed action!

Date: _____

Day 1: Motivate with Values

Debbie: *I try to take ten thousand steps daily. I feel pride on the days I make my goal. But some days the battery on my fitness tracker runs out, or I forget to put it on, and I don't bother to take the extra steps that would get me all the way to my goal. Who cares if I sit around all day? Steps I don't track don't "count," right? But if I go on a long walk with my family, or take a hike in the mountains, I'm intrinsically motivated because movement is tied to something more important to me than a number. Taking steps can be an arbitrary external goal, or it can be connected to my values.*

Say your roommate wanted to motivate you to clean your dishes. She could pay you $1 per dish. Will this work? You bet! But what happens when she can't pay, or she's over it?

Committed action takes a different approach to motivating behavior change: instead of relying on extrinsic (outside) motivators, it relies on values for inspiration. What you care about deep inside is intrinsically motivating and always with you, and therefore it is more sustainable in the long run than gold stars or fleeting praise.

What if you decided to wash dishes because you cared about contributing to your household? You may not jump with joy at the task, but you're likely to keep doing the dishes, even when your roommate's not around. As you'll learn, affirming your value of contributing could also have broader impacts on your life beyond clean dishes.

Today you're going to identify reasons to change that are personal, chosen by you, and always with you.

ACT Daily Writing: Digging for Values

Let's uncover your intrinsic motivation for change. Write down three changes you'd like to make.

1. _____
2. _____
3. _____

Why might these changes really matter to you? How would they enhance your life? What would make them worth it even when they feel hard?

_____
_____
_____
_____

Distill your thinking even more. What are three values underlying the changes you want to make?

_____
_____
_____

Try It Now: Valued Action

Consider the values you wrote above. Translate one of them into the smallest committed action you could take right now and do it. For example:
- If you value caring for your body, take a moment to stretch.

- If you care about the environment, reuse something.
- If you care about being loving, give someone a call or a hug.

ACT in My Life: Today's Values, Goals, Reflections

_____
_____
_____
_____
_____
_____
_____
_____
_____
_____
_____
_____
_____

Today's Practice

Build your intrinsic motivation by using the savoring skill from Week 2. Really pay attention to how good it feels to act on your values. Notice when you act in ways that align with what you care about, and when you do so, take in the satisfying feeling of valued action.

Date: _____

Day 2: Actions Not Outcomes

Diana: *My family likes to make salsa in a* molcajete, *a Mexican mortar and pestle made from volcanic rock that we use to grind peppers, tomatoes, onions, garlic, and cilantro. Our salsa is less predictable than store-bought, but the result isn't really the reason we make it this way; it's the process of involving our kids, working with our hands, and exploring a different culture that we value.*

ACT is a behavioral psychology, meaning its focus is on the behaviors you can do with your hands and feet more than on the outcomes these behaviors produce. Keeping your attention on actions instead of end points will help you sustain a behavior, especially when it's messy. Why? We have a lot less control over outcomes than we do over our behavior. If you only focus on results when learning a new skill, you'll likely get discouraged when you fumble, or possibly stop doing it once you reach your goal. As Diana's friend who teaches a noisy high school band class says to people who complain about the noise: "This is what learning sounds like!"

Behavioral research also shows us that small, slow change is the most sustainable type. According to Stanford professor and habit guru B.J. Fogg (2019), motivation comes in "waves," and it's best to design habits that you'll do even when motivation is low. Although it can feel exciting to make a big jump, drastic changes can be unsustainable. When you use what Fogg calls "tiny habits" to grow a new behavior you're more likely to keep at it even when you're weary and life gets busy.

ACT Daily Writing: Make It Smaller

Write down a behavior you've been trying to grow.

Are you focusing on any particular outcomes (instead of action)?

_____
_____
_____

Take the behavior you want to grow and commit to an action that is so small you're certain you can do it. For example, if you wrote "Meditate for ten minutes a day," how about three minutes instead? Rewrite the modified behavior.

_____
_____
_____

Try It Now: Imaginal Practice

Like a basketball player imagining shooting hoops before bed, you can use the skill of imagery to "practice" a values-based action in your mind. Mentally rehearsing a behavior helps

encode it in your mind and later recall the skill in real life (McKay and West 2016). Picture yourself:
- Taking a small values-based action
- Accepting difficult emotions, urges, and thoughts that show up for you
- Continuing to take small steps toward your values

ACT in My Life: Today's Values, Goals, Reflections

_____
_____
_____
_____
_____
_____
_____
_____
_____
_____
_____

Today's Practice

Pick three small values-based actions to commit to today. Write them down, let go of their outcome, and focus on taking action!

_____

_____

_____

Date: _____

Day 3: Obstacles to Change

Diana: *I have a drawer of half-filled journals. Each represents a time when I aimed to "start again" at daily journaling. Inevitably after a few weeks of daily writing I lose motivation, stop, and store the journal away unfinished. For a long time I felt like a failure every time I looked at that drawer. Why couldn't I keep my commitment to daily journaling? What's wrong with me? Now I see the drawer differently. It's packed with my commitment to journaling. It shows all the times I had the stamina to start again and holds my treasured collection of imperfect, ongoing committed action.*

Learning a new skill involves facing both internal and external obstacles. For example, if you can fry an egg, you overcame many obstacles as you learned this skill. External obstacles may have included things like being tall enough to reach the stove and having eggs in the house. Internal obstacles may have included things like the fear of burning yourself and breaking the yolk by accident.

Whereas external obstacles are best tackled with problem solving, internal obstacles benefit from ACT processes, such as acceptance, being present, perspective taking, cognitive defusion, and compassion.

Today we're going to explore some of the obstacles you face in taking committed action. We'll unpack past attempts to change and point you to skills that may help you when you get off track.

ACT Daily Writing: Obstacles

Write down a behavior you've tried to change in the past but "failed" at, according to your mind.

⎯⎯⎯⎯⎯⎯⎯⎯⎯⎯⎯⎯⎯⎯⎯⎯⎯

What external obstacles made this behavior more difficult?

How might you overcome these obstacles in the future?

_____

_____

What about internal obstacles? What TEAMS—thoughts, emotions, action tendencies, memories, or sensations (see Week 4)—made this behavior more difficult?

_____

_____

What ACT strategies might you use to flexibly respond to these internal obstacles? For example, would it help to defuse from your thoughts, accept your emotions, or practice self-compassion?

Try It Now: Feeling Pride

Committed action can activate feelings of mastery and pride. Think about a behavior that makes you proud. Choose one that can be hard for you but is linked to your values. Now think about the many times that you faced obstacles yet returned to the behavior. Recall the feeling of pride and mastery when you took that committed action.

ACT in My Life: Today's Values, Goals, Reflections

_____
_____
_____
_____
_____
_____
_____
_____
_____
_____

Today's Practice

Greet your obstacles to committed action by, first, preparing for and problem solving the external obstacles, and, second, meeting your internal obstacles with ACT skills. When you face an obstacle today, see it as an opportunity to build strength, adapt, and grow.

Date: _____

Day 4: Creating Contexts

The context we live in shapes our behavior. Although a lot of contexts are out of your control, there's a lot you can do to structure your environment to support your valued actions. One way to shape context is to design cues that trigger the behaviors you want to grow. Behavior occurs in a three-step sequence:

Cue → Action → Consequence

Cues are what spark a behavior.

Debbie: *When the TV is on, I inevitably start watching, even though I don't like to spend much time that way. I keep the only TV in my house in an extra bedroom in my basement, so that TV-watching becomes an infrequent event. Removing the cue of the TV structures my environment in a way that decreases an undesired behavior.*

Here are a few helpful tips for designing cues for a new behavior:

- **Structure your environment:** Make it easier to engage in the behaviors you want to grow and harder to engage in the ones you don't. For example, charge your phone far away from your bedroom at bedtime, store your alcohol out of sight in a closed cabinet, put your sunscreen in a visible location.
- **"Pancake" your habits:** Just like you stack pancakes, layer a new behavior—or behaviors—on top of something you already do daily. For example, if you drink coffee in the morning (existing habit), and you want to remember to take your medications in the morning, place your meds by the coffee maker (cue) and take them with your coffee (pancake habit).
- **Do your future self a favor:** Your motivation will inevitably fluctuate. Try designing contexts that will make it easier for your future, unmotivated self to engage in a valued behavior. For example, if you want to eat healthier but feel too tired to make food after work,

batch-cook healthy food on the weekend.

Today you get to design contexts that spark your values-based behaviors. Tomorrow we'll add some consequences to keep the flame alive.

ACT Daily Writing: Spark the Flame

Think about a behavior you want to build. How can you structure your environment to spark this behavior?

_____
_____

Pancake your habits. What daily activities can you stack your new behavior on top of?

_____
_____

How can you do your future self a favor by making this behavior easier to start in the days ahead?

ACT in My Life: Today's Values, Goals, Reflections

Today's Practice

Prepare your environment to support your valued behaviors. Create cues—change your living environment, set up reminders, or rearrange your technology—that spark future success.

Date: _____

Day 5: Will Wake for Coffee!

Debbie: *I used to have a snooze habit. I'd hit that tempting button five or six times before getting up most mornings, avoiding the unpleasantness of starting my day. I wanted to start getting up earlier, so I focused on reinforcing aspects of the morning—a cup of coffee and quiet time to write or read—to change my habit. Now when my alarm goes off, I think about the meaningful moments, and the jolt of caffeine, that await me downstairs and get out of bed without hitting snooze even once.*

Yesterday you focused on creating cues to support new behaviors. Today, let's focus on reinforcing the behaviors you want to grow, like how Debbie reinforces waking up with coffee. Going back to the cue-action-consequence sequence, whether you start a behavior depends on cues, but whether you repeat it depends on consequences.

Your brain tends to focus more on short-term consequences over long-term ones because it evolved from ancestors whose survival depended on it. If your ancestors prioritized short-term consequences (Will this berry kill me?) over longer-term ones (Does this berry have the right blend of antioxidants?), they lived to pass on their genes.

But in today's world it's the ability to stick with discomfort and focus on the long term that supports our most important goals. The good news is that you can use newer parts of your brain to reorient yourself toward your values and long-term goals. For example, you can deliberately design consequences to reinforce your long-term goals, track your progress, and focus your attention on savoring the benefits of your values-based actions.

Try out the following with a behavior you want to grow:
- *Imagine* yourself reaching your long-term values-based goals to make short-term steps more reinforcing
- *Track* your new behavior by writing it down or by using a habit app on your phone (self-monitoring

increases awareness and is reinforcing)
- *Focus attention* on your values while accepting some unpleasant experiences in the short term
- *Savor* the feeling of building competency and creating meaning

ACT Daily Writing: Short Term, Long Term

Think of something that you're currently working on changing. What's hard about engaging in this new behavior in the short term? What are the long-term benefits to making this change?

_____
_____
_____

What values do you want to remind yourself of and savor when doing your new behavior? Make a list.

ACT in My Life: Today's Values, Goals, Reflections

Today's Practice

Create consequences to reinforce the behaviors you want to increase. Set up a way to track a new behavior, and when you engage in it picture your longer-term goals and remind yourself that you are doing this for a reason.

Date:_____

Day 6: Your Dream Team

Diana: *I love my private practice. It's empowering to be my own boss, create my own schedule, and pick out my own throw pillows. But by working alone I miss out on the creativity, accountability, and collective strength of a group. Podcasting with Debbie and our colleagues fills that need. My cohosts give me the courage to take professional risks, carry the load when I'm exhausted, and weave their ideas with mine to create something better than I could have alone.*

Sometimes you might set a goal and tackle it alone. That can work fine. But when you're trying to expand an important area of your life, support from others can help. People thrive in supportive networks, and activating the social engagement systems of your brain contributes to the positive emotions of affiliation and feeling secure (Gilbert 2017). Kelly McGonigal (2019) describes the synchronicity and delight that people share on sports teams and while engaging in group exercise as "collective joy." What's more, research is clear that having support increases your chances of successfully changing a behavior (Greaney et al. 2018).

There are a lot of ways to build support:
- Recruit a friend or family member to join you in reaching a values-based goal.
- Join a group that's already doing something that you want to do.
- Find an online community that has shared values.
- Tell friends and family about the changes you're making.

You can then use your social group for accountability, support, and problem solving when those pesky internal and external obstacles arise. Working with others can enhance relationship values and make behavior change a lot more fun, both added benefits.

ACT Daily Writing: Who's on Your Team?

What person, or group of people, can support you in meeting your goals?

What support do you want from them?

_____
_____

If you and your support group were members of a team, what roles would each person play? Who's best for keeping you accountable, teaching you new skills, helping you face obstacles, or being a compassionate coach?

_____
_____
_____
_____
_____
_____

Try It Now: Team Huddle

Imagine the members of your team huddling around you in support. Take in the feeling of being cared for and held by this group. When you feel alone in your behavior-change efforts, use this image for encouragement and strength.

ACT in My Life: Today's Values, Goals, Reflections

_____
_____
_____
_____
_____
_____
_____
_____
_____
_____

Today's Practice

Build your support network by joining an online community or reaching out to a current friend or family member and letting them know what you're working on.

Date: _____

Day 7: Your Action Plan

Debbie: *When I was a young student, I experienced a lot of anguish trying to figure out my future career path. I felt pressure to make the "right" decision, imagining I would choose a profession, work hard, and go straight from point A to point B—and stay there. In reality, my career path has meandered through direction changes, unexpected opportunities, and setbacks—with many ups and downs along the way. I could never have predicted how things would unfold. The journey itself has been empowering, and I'm curious to discover what will happen next!*

The in-flight screen mapping a trip from LA to New York shows a straight line from takeoff to landing. But this is not the airplane's real path. The plane will head south to avoid storms, north to catch a tailwind, and circle above its destination while waiting for an open gate. If you've learned anything this week, it's that committed action is not a straight path, and it has no real destination. It's a series of ongoing, values-guided behaviors that are never truly finished! Today you will put all of your committed action practices together to launch a flexible flight path toward a long-term goal in a domain you care about.

We hope you use your flight path as a guide and adjust course as needed, just like a skilled pilot would do.

ACT Daily Writing: ACT Daily Action Plan

Use the skills you learned this week to write an action plan for an area of life you care deeply about. Use this plan as a template any time you want to put your values into action! (This template is available for download at this book's website: http://www.newharbinger.com/47377. See the back of the book for more details.)

Step 1: What change do you want to make in an important domain (such as family, romantic partner, work, community, leisure, physical self-care, creative expression, spirituality, or the environment)?

___

Step 2: What values motivate this change?

___

Step 3: What actions can you take to demonstrate your values?

___

Step 4: What inner and outer obstacles do you anticipate? What problem-solving skills and ACT processes will help you overcome them?

___

Step 5: What contexts and cues can you create to support your actions?

___

Step 6: How will you reinforce your actions? What could you do to keep the flame alive?

___

Step 7: Who's on your support team?

_____

Step 8: How can you flexibly respond when you find yourself off course?

_____

ACT in My Life: Today's Values, Goals, Reflections

_____
_____
_____
_____
_____
_____
_____
_____
_____
_____
_____
_____
_____
_____
_____

Today's Practice

Try out your action plan today. Be flexible and adapt as needed to execute your plan. And take time to revise your plan based on how things go.

Final Reflections

This week you learned about some of the behavioral science related to making behavior changes stick. You learned how to self-motivate with values and create contexts that will cue new behavior. You learned the importance of reinforcing your actions and building a support team to keep you motivated over the long term. Finally, you created an action plan. We hope you keep these ideas in your back pocket to use again in the future. Next week we'll focus on integrating all that you've learned in order to take your behavioral skills to the next level. You will go beyond focusing on your individual well-being to using ACT processes to contribute to the well-being of all.

Week 8

Flexible Integration—Hive Mind

When Diana became a beekeeper, she learned to give her hive a singular name, such as Hadley or Henry. Honeybees are such an interconnected species that the fifty thousand or more of them in a hive are considered a single superorganism. They're *ultrasocial*, meaning they cooperate and depend on each other to survive. Some bees guard the hive's door while others care for the young, and they "festoon" by joining legs to reach the low spots when making honeycombs.

ACT works similarly. The core processes of ACT are interrelated and work best when practiced together. Over the last seven weeks you've worked your way through the core processes of ACT, one at a time. But you've probably already noticed that they overlap. When you get present, as you did in Week 2, you started to notice your buzzing thoughts, which you then defused from in Week 3. When you explored acceptance and emotional willingness in Week 4, you probably unveiled your deepest values (Week 6). And on and on it goes!

When woven together, the core processes of ACT create a humming hive of psychological flexibility.

This week, we're going take your daily ACT practice to the next level by learning more about how these processes enrich each other and can be applied beyond oneself. Just like bees, humans are an ultrasocial species (Tomasello 2014). We cooperate, work best in groups, and depend on one another. As you work on integrating the ACT processes this week, you can use them to go beyond yourself and promote a kinder, more flexible, and socially responsive world.

Date: _____

Day 1: Take Stock

Whether you started this journal eight weeks or eight months ago, we hope it has helped you live more from your heart, be pushed around less by your head, and take action with your feet. Today is your chance to go back through your work, reflect, and review what was most impactful. You might notice that some areas were especially important in your own personal growth. You might also consider which practices you want to keep working on as you move forward.

Below is an overview of the processes you've been working on, to refresh your memory. Take stock of your meaningful, hard work!

Week 1. Compassion, self-care, and intentional use of time: you cultivated a compassionate inner advisor, kinder self-care practices, and more intentional use of time.

Week 2. Being present: you learned to move from autopilot to savoring the present moment.

Week 3. Cognitive defusion: you stepped back from your chatty mind, wacky thoughts, and judgments and learned to water more helpful thoughts.

Week 4. Acceptance: you learned how emotional avoidance keeps you stuck, and how to open up to all of your inner experiences.

Week 5. Perspective taking: you gained a new view of self-stories and explored the possibility of stepping out of these stories into timelessness, connection, and belonging.

Week 6. Values: you explored what matters most to you in important domains of your life and the actions that reflect your deepest caring.

Week 7. Committed action: you learned about the science of behavioral psychology and how to take small steps toward meaningful change.

ACT Daily Writing: Let's Review

Go back through your journal and review your writing. For each section, reflect on the most impactful lessons, and note the practices you want to carry forward.

Compassion, self-care, and intentional use of time: _____

Being present: _____

Cognitive defusion: _____

Acceptance: _____

Perspective taking: _____

Values: _____

Committed action: _____

Try It Now: And ... Breathe

Take in three slow breaths. One breath for your past self who has done this courageous work. One breath for your current self, practicing psychological flexibility right now. And a last breath for your future self, committed to psychological flexibility and the change to come.

ACT in My Life: Today's Values, Goals, Reflections

_____
_____
_____
_____
_____
_____
_____
_____
_____

Today's Practice

Choose some practices from your journal review to practice again today. See if you can point out the different ACT processes working together. For example, if you choose to pause and take in the perspective of another, can you notice how you are tapping into the present moment and your values?

Date: _____

Day 2: Adapting with Psychological Flexibility

Psychological flexibility is about adapting over time and as circumstances change. The ability to adapt is essential for our survival, allowing us to:
- Take in new information
- Hold our assumptions lightly
- Let go of unhelpful patterns
- Weather unavoidable emotions
- Learn and grow
- Adjust course when necessary to do what's most effective

Debbie: *Some of my most meaningful work involves helping the "helpers," such as health care professionals and caregivers who do the important work of caring for others, even in the face of extraordinary stress, adversity, trauma, and grief. These helpers put aside their own needs for others, navigate unfathomable scenarios, and make life-and-death decisions. It can be exhausting and depleting. As a "helper of helpers," my work is to* *support them in adapting flexibly, tending to their own well-being, reconnecting with purpose, and finding personal growth in the face of it all.*

We can't change unchangeable circumstances, but we can do our best to adapt flexibly using ACT processes. At times, flexible change can happen slowly, such as you growing to accept your parents as flawed humans, or rapidly, such as first responders adapting to the new demands of a disaster. Sometimes it's more adaptive to *not* adapt to a new circumstance that goes against your values (such as remaining in a toxic or abusive situation) but to remain firm in your stance. And the outside world may not always praise the changes you make that move you toward your values. ACT is a personal and deep inquiry into how you want to use your time on this planet, and then organizing your actions around that.

> Part of the reason ACT is so wonderful is that you decide what really matters to you, and you can live those values every day.

ACT Daily Writing: Adapt and Grow

Explore some of the ways you've flexibly adapted over time. When have you become more accepting? More forgiving? More flexible? Wiser? Take a moment to appreciate (and write about) your growth.

_____
_____
_____
_____
_____

What unhelpful old beliefs and patterns have stuck around? How would you like to further evolve?

_____
_____
_____
_____

Try It Now: The History in Your Hands

Take a look at your palm. Make a fist and open it again. Notice where the lines are. These lines and wrinkles are the history of your hand's many movements over time. What have you held, touched, made, and written to form these lines? What do you want to do with this hand today?

ACT in My Life: Today's Values, Goals, Reflections

_____
_____
_____
_____
_____
_____
_____
_____
_____
_____
_____

Today's Practice

Today see yourself as an ever-evolving, adaptable being. Notice how you navigate life's unexpected challenges. See if you can be more flexible and wiser in your life.

Date: _____

Day 3: Sidetracked from Values

Diana: *In third grade I cheated in a multiplication contest. My gut still drops when I think about my teacher announcing that I had won. She gave me a pin that said, "The truth will set you free." I don't know if she gave me that particular pin because she knew I had cheated, but I'll always know what it feels like to stray from my truth. Now when I feel that same gut check, I'm grateful for the inner reminder to reorient.*

We all stray from our values sometimes. When you're stressed, caught up in a craving or in striving, or challenged by adversity, there's a good chance you'll lose sight of your values and get stuck in unhelpful patterns. When strong emotions and sticky thoughts push you around, it can be all too easy to get sidetracked and react impulsively:

- Your partner annoys you, so you say something hurtful, even though you care about treating her with respect.
- At the end of a hard day, you numb out with substances, technology, or food when you could instead use the time productively.
- You procrastinate on important projects you're worried about.
- You close off from a friend who needs support because the conversation might feel sad or painful.
- You don't read articles about racism, the environment, or politics because you might feel guilty, sad, or angry.

Even in hard times it's possible to choose how to respond based on the person you'd most like to be. You can always pause, notice your thoughts and emotions, ask yourself how you'd respond at your best, and make that choice. By doing this, you can connect with meaning, even in the most stressful of life's circumstances. And when you get it wrong, all you can do is keep moving forward and do better next time.

ACT Daily Writing: Sidetracked

Write about a struggle that sidetracks you from being the person you want to be. What tend to be your automatic reactions when your thoughts and emotions push you around in this struggle? What choices could you make that would be more consistent with your values?

_____
_____
_____
_____

ACT in My Life: Today's Values, Goals, Reflections

_____
_____
_____
_____
_____
_____
_____
_____

Today's Practice

Pay special attention in the hard moments today—perhaps a stressful moment at work or school, a moment of boredom or tedium, or a struggle you encounter. Pause there and see what you notice. What habits or urges show up? See these moments as opportunities to choose a values-consistent response.

Date: _____

Day 4: Get Uncomfortable, on Purpose

Debbie: *Years ago, while teaching a lecture course at Harvard, I included a unit on racism. I felt like I was out of my league; as a white woman, my experience with racism has been limited by my privileged perspective. Who am I to teach others about something I don't fully understand myself? I wondered. I was afraid I'd mess up and, worse, offend some of my students. I worked hard to prepare and stumbled through awkwardly, unsure whether I was up for the task. I probably got some things wrong, but I'm glad I took the risk. I value speaking out about all forms of oppression, including racism, and feel proud that I taught a course about something important, even if I felt uncomfortable while doing it.*

As you've learned in your ACT practice, it's natural to want to turn away from discomfort. But the magic happens when we turn toward it. A lot of self-help books are about self-improvement: *How can I get stronger, richer, more productive, thinner, better?* But ACT is different.

ACT is about getting out of our own way so we can show up and move toward something that matters more than personal comfort or success.

It takes psychological flexibility for real transformation to occur in your life, and on this planet. To move forward and do the right thing, sometimes we need to step back from inflexible beliefs and enter into difficult feelings, conversations, and actions. Whether you're moved to start some uncomfortable conversations, take action toward social justice, or try something new, you can stock up on your ACT tools and put what you've learned to good use.

ACT Daily Writing: Fuel Up with Courage and Action

Identify an area that's important to you, one in which you tend to shy away from conversations or actions because they're uncomfortable.

_____

What TEAMS (see Week 4) show up as you consider taking a step toward your values in this area?

_____
_____

What ACT skills can you fuel up with to get out of your own way?

_____
_____

What difficult emotions and sensations are you willing to accept in order to take action?

_____

What action steps can you take that would reflect courage, dignity, and love in this area?

ACT in My Life: Today's Values, Goals, Reflections

_____
_____
_____
_____
_____
_____
_____
_____
_____
_____

Today's Practice

Today, choose to get uncomfortable in the service of your values. Actively choose an area that matters to you and try:

- Starting a difficult conversation and staying in it longer than usual
- Exposing yourself to uncomfortable media or other perspectives to broaden your point of view
- Taking an action step out of your comfort zone that will make a difference
- Using psychological flexibility skills to empower yourself to do something that matters in the world

Date: _____

Day 5: Our Common Humanity

Recognizing our shared, common humanity promotes understanding, forgiveness, and kindness. A foundational stance in ACT is that we're all human—therapists and clients alike. We all make mistakes, get caught in all-too-human struggles, and are doing the best we can.

Diana: *One day while rushing out of a parking lot I pulled into the sidewalk in front of a jogger, almost hitting her. I rolled down the window to see if she was okay. She waved with a look of understanding and said, "I've done that before." The jogger's unexpected kindness motivated me more than any dirty look would have. I still think about her and use her mantra when a friend needs to cancel plans, or my kid spills something on the carpet. "I understand. I've done that before."*

Psychological flexibility can support *prosocial behaviors*—behaviors that benefit others and society as a whole (Atkins, Wilson, and Hayes 2019; Biglan 2015):

- With perspective taking and values, we can choose to respond with more kindness, forgiveness, and cooperation.
- With compassion and acceptance, we can hold the pain of being hurt or disappointed even when others are at their worst.
- With cognitive defusion and perspective taking, we can express empathy and give others the benefit of the doubt.
- By being present and taking committed action, we can offer good wishes and a warm heart, even in the most difficult conversations.

In return, prosocial behaviors can improve relationships, making us happier and healthier (Diener and Seligman 2002; Holt-Lunstad, Robles, and Sbarra 2017). Kind and generous behaviors unite us as a species (Lynch 2018), triggering our nervous system to make us feel safe with others (Porges 2011).

Prosocial actions, even small ones, create greater human thriving and might just make the world a better place for all of us.

Today, let's build a better world by acting prosocially, together.

ACT Daily Writing: Loving-Kindness

Which people or groups do you feel most loving toward right now?

_____
_____

And which people or groups do you feel less connected with, or more judgment toward, right now?

_____
_____

How might you build more kindness, empathy, forgiveness, and connection related to people in both categories?

_____

What kind actions might you take today?

_____
_____

ACT in My Life: Today's Values, Goals, Reflections

_____
_____
_____
_____
_____
_____

Today's Practice

Take some mindful breaths and read this beautiful meditation from *Awakening Together* by Larry Yang (2017, 151):

May I be as loving in this moment as possible.

If I cannot be loving in this moment,
may I be kind;

If I cannot be kind,
may I be nonjudgmental;

If I cannot be nonjudgmental,
may I not cause harm;

And if I cannot not cause harm,
may I cause the least amount of harm possible.

Date: _____

Day 6: Bigger than Me

Psychology tends to focus on individuals, underemphasizing the cultural and systemic contexts in which we live. ACT has the potential to do more than help with the suffering that's inside each of us by considering the broader cultural, political, and economic systems that contribute to suffering in the world. ACT encourages us to consider our lives in a broad context and to look beyond what lies within (Hayes 2019).

Debbie: *Before I started my clinical psychology training, I worked for an anonymous peer-support hotline for students. A female graduate student from another country called in, upset and in tears because her powerful male academic advisor was sexually harassing her. I recommended that she seek therapy to help her cope with her fear and sadness. In hindsight, I was completely wrong. I missed the real problem: she was in a toxic situation and the first priority was caring for her* *safety. I would respond very differently today. I would acknowledge that her emotional reaction was valid and support her in finding ways to protect herself.*

As therapists we've learned that people find greater fulfillment if they're able to step outside their own self-focused point of view and connect with something bigger than themselves, perhaps by forming close, connected relationships with others, collaborating with a group (Atkins, Wilson, and Hayes 2019), contributing to a social cause, or nurturing children (Biglan 2015). It can be hard to make this leap if we have tunnel vision, focusing on only our own immediate problems. This broadening of contexts is where perspective taking meets values.

ACT Daily Writing: Something Bigger

Reflect back on the values you identified in Week 6. Which ones are tied to something bigger than you, such as giving, caring, groups, social causes, and so forth? What systems do you most want to work toward changing? How can you step outside yourself and do something that matters in the world?

___

Try It Now: Metta Meditation

Diana's neighbor, a practicing Buddhist, once gave her a note card with the following meditation to recite at night, when Diana was having a hard time. It reminds us that our well-being is interconnected with that of others.

Repeat the following meditation out loud or to yourself.

May I be one with myself.

May I be free from suffering.

May I be at peace.

May _____ [name of someone you love] be one with themselves.

May _____ [name of someone you love] be free from suffering.

May _____ [name of someone you love] be at peace.

May we all be one with ourselves.

May we be free from suffering.

May we be at peace.

ACT in My Life: Today's Values, Goals, Reflections

_____
_____
_____
_____
_____
_____
_____
_____
_____
_____
_____
_____
_____
_____

Today's Practice

Today, notice your connection to the bigger whole and make a contribution of some kind. Take a small action that contributes to something bigger than you.

Date: _____

Day 7: Your ACT Daily Life

Diana: *In between having my two sons I gave birth to a stillborn boy. After I delivered him, the nurses asked me if I wanted to hold him. It was psychological flexibility training that gave me the courage to say yes. As my husband and I received his tiny body wrapped in a blanket, we breathed in the intensity of love and loss. I think about that moment often. I wonder about the person who made his little blanket—what life experience motivated such an act? I feel gratitude for the nurses who wisely encouraged us to take our time, and for my husband who joined me in feeling fully. ACT is about the willingness to step into moments like these—exposing ourselves to vulnerability so we can open ourselves to love.*

When learning to ride a bike, there's a moment when a child forgets to focus on balancing, pedaling, and steering and the act of riding becomes an embodied knowing. Today is your last day of *ACT*

Daily, and now is the time to put all the pieces together and ride with an inner knowing and embodiment of ACT.

This journal has been focused on applying ACT directly to your sometimes mundane, other times difficult, and hopefully satisfying life as it is. As you move through life, we hope you continue to use what you've learned here to turn suffering into meaning, impermanence into a reminder of what matters most, and your deepest longings into action. As bell hooks writes, "Our sufferings do not magically end; instead we are able to wisely alchemically recycle them. They become abundant waste that we use to make new growth possible" (2001, 80–81).

ACT Daily Writing: Your Future Self

Looking ahead, and knowing that you will face times of loss and change, what would you like to tell your future self about using ACT?

Knowing that you will face mundane, boring, and simple days, what would you like to tell your future self about using ACT?

_____
_____
_____

Knowing that you will face moments when it's both uncomfortable and important to use your voice or to take action, what would you like to tell your future self about using ACT?

_____
_____

ACT in My Life: Today's Values, Goals, Reflections

_____
_____
_____
_____
_____
_____
_____
_____
_____
_____
_____
_____

Today's Practice

Today, as you move forward with your life beyond *ACT Daily,* commit to continuing the work you've done. Think about your next steps and ways you might remind your future self of how far you've come.

Final Reflections

This week you took your psychological flexibility beyond the realm of your personal well-being. From a stance of hive mind, you learned how your everyday moves can have an impact on a greater whole. In *A Liberated Mind,* Steven Hayes closes, "With each person who learns [ACT] skills, the culture evolves just a little bit. Human communication softens; human connection grows" (2019, 386). In that same vein, we wish you more softening, more connection, more growth, and more freedom in the days to come.

The Labyrinth Ahead

Diana: *When my clients end therapy with me, I often give them a pewter symbol of a labyrinth. It's a physical offering that represents our work together and the work to come. Like a maze, a labyrinth winds back and forth, but unlike a maze a labyrinth has no dead end and is not designed to confuse. There's no "getting out" of a labyrinth. Instead, as long as you keep moving forward you find your way to the center.*

Every twist and turn of a labyrinth brings one closer to its center. Living the ACT processes daily is like following a labyrinth: There will be times when it feels like you're just skimming the outer edge of the spiral, far from the center and not making progress. Other times, you'll feel like you're on the fast track to freedom.

No matter your circumstances, you will likely experience periods of positive change followed by stagnation or loss. If you've felt anxious, angry, or blue, those feelings will come back. If you've struggled to sustain a change, the struggle will show up again. If you're in recovery from an addiction, you will likely face the twists and turns of urges and lapses many times. And so on.

It's how we respond to life's inevitable twists and turns that's important. The labyrinth of ACT teaches us that it's always possible to keep moving ahead flexibly, responding to challenges in an open, aware, and values-consistent way. As you move along the labyrinth ahead, ACTing daily calls for you to be open, aware, and engaged (Hayes, Strosahl, and Wilson 2012):

- **Open:** Can you gently welcome all your feelings, thoughts, and sensations?
- **Aware:** Are you aware of the TEAMS that are hooking you, and of what matters most to you right now?
- **Engaged:** Are you living your values through your actions in this moment?

Not only does life change over time, you'll find that the ACT processes themselves are more fluid than stagnant. None of the processes are fixed in the sense that you do them once and you're done.

- *Being present* means finding your center in this moment only to notice how quickly you lose it again.
- *Cognitive defusion* means repeatedly unhooking from unhelpful thoughts, as your chattering mind will never stop.
- *Acceptance* is not a permanent state, rather it's choosing to turn toward your full experience over and over again.
- *Perspective taking* means observing all of your experiences as impermanent.
- *Values* aren't something you do once and you're done. They are a direction you continue to head in for a lifetime.
- *Committed action* requires you to respond with kindness and to move forward when you inevitably slip back into old habits and automatic behaviors.

Putting ACT into practice is a lifelong journey; the processes become part of your life when you live them consistently over time. With practice, it gets easier to notice when there's work to do. Here are some pointers for keeping the ACT processes alive when you're feeling stuck:

- **Do an awareness check:** Practice *one eye in* (What is happening in my body and mind?) and *one eye out* (What is happening in the moment around me?).
- **Pause:** Open up to your emotions and thoughts when you catch yourself struggling. See what shifts.
- **Take perspective:** Step back from what's in front of you and expand your point of view to include the bigger picture.
- **Reconnect with values:** Revisit your life motto from Week 6 and compare how you're doing with how you want to live. Readjust as necessary.

With these tools you can keep inching forward, at your own pace, toward your own chosen values. And, if you're like lots of people and could use a little help with organization, we crafted a daily planner based on the six ACT processes. It's available for download at this book's website: http://www.newharbinger.com/47377. (See the back of the book for more details.) *The ACT processes are always available to you; it's up to you to put them into practice in your life.*

Thank you for choosing *ACT Daily*. We hope you take what you learned here and use it to keep building a life that's most meaningful to you. May you enjoy the journey!

Additional Resources

Learn More About ACT

A Liberated Mind: How to Pivot Toward What Matters by Steven Hayes

The Association for Contextual Behavioral Science at https://www.contextualscience.org

Psychologists Off the Clock podcast at https://www.offtheclockpsych.com

Apply ACT for Specific Groups

Be Mighty: A Woman's Guide to Liberation from Anxiety, Worry, and Stress Using Mindfulness and Acceptance by Jill A. Stoddard

End the Insomnia Struggle: A Step-by-Step Guide to Help You Get to Sleep and Stay Asleep by Colleen Ehrnstrom and Alisha L. Brosse

Living with Your Body and Other Things You Hate: How to Let Go of Your Struggle with Body Image Using Acceptance and Commitment Therapy by Emily Sandoz and Troy DuFrene

Mastering Adulthood: Go Beyond Adulting to Become an Emotional Grown-Up by Lara E. Fielding

The Wisdom to Know the Difference: An Acceptance and Commitment Therapy Workbook for Overcoming Substance Abuse by Kelly G. Wilson and Troy DuFrene

Your Life, Your Way: Acceptance and Commitment Therapy Skills to Help Teens Manage Emotions and Build Resilience by Joseph V. Ciarrochi and Louise L. Hayes

Foster Compassion and Kindness

Awakening Together: The Spiritual Practice of Inclusivity and Community by Larry Yang

The Compassionate Mind: A New Approach to Life's Challenges by Paul Gilbert

How to Be Nice to Yourself: The Everyday Guide to Self-Compassion—Effective Strategies to Increase Self-Love and Acceptance by Laura Silberstein-Tirch

The Mindful Path to Self-Compassion: Freeing Yourself from Destructive Thoughts and Emotions by Christopher K. Germer

The Self-Care Prescription: Powerful Solutions to Manage Stress, Reduce Anxiety, and Increase Well-Being by Robyn Gobin

Start Where You Are: A Guide to Compassionate Living by Pema Chödrön

An Open-Hearted Life: Transformative Methods for Compassionate Living from a Clinical Psychologist and a Buddhist Nun by Russell Kolts and Thubten Chödrön

Build Awareness

Being Peace by Thich Nhat Hanh

Just One Thing: Developing a Buddha Brain One Simple Practice at a Time by Rick Hanson

Mindful of Race: Transforming Racism from the Inside Out by Ruth King

Slow: Simple Living for a Frantic World by Brook McAlary

The Untethered Soul: The Journey Beyond Yourself by Michael A. Singer

Cultivate Acceptance

All About Love: New Visions by bell hooks

Neurodharma: New Science, Ancient Wisdom, and Seven Practices of the Highest Happiness by Rick Hanson

Radical Acceptance: Embracing Your Life with the Heart of a Buddha by Tara Brach

When Things Fall Apart: Heart Advice for Difficult Times by Pema Chödrön

Find Meaning and Purpose

Man's Search for Meaning by Viktor E. Frankl

The New Happiness: Practices for Spiritual Growth and Living with Intention by Matthew McKay and Jeffrey C. Wood

Playing Big: Practical Wisdom for Women Who Want to Speak Up, Create, and Lead by Tara Mohr

The Power of Meaning: Finding Fulfillment in a World Obsessed with Happiness by Emily Esfahani Smith

Prosocial: Using Evolutionary Science to Build Productive, Equitable, and Collaborative Groups by Paul W.B.

Atkins, David Sloan Wilson, and Steven C. Hayes

Inspiration for Behavior Change

Healthy Habits Suck: How to Get Off the Couch and Live a Healthy Life ... Even If You Don't Want To by Dayna Lee-Baggley

The Joy of Movement: How Exercise Helps Us Find Happiness, Hope, Connection, and Courage by Kelly McGonigal

Off the Clock: Feel Less Busy While Getting More Done by Laura Vanderkam

The Power of Small: Making Tiny Changes When Everything Feels Too Much by Aisling Leonard-Curtin and Trish Leonard-Curtin

Tiny Habits: The Small Changes That Change Everything by B.J. Fogg

Recommended for Therapists

Acceptance and Commitment Therapy: The Process and Practice of Mindful Change, 2nd edition, by Steven C. Hayes, Kirk D. Strosahl, and Kelly G. Wilson

The Essential Guide to the ACT Matrix: A Step-by-Step Approach to Using the ACT Matrix Model in Clinical Practice by Kevin L. Polk, Benjamin Schoendorff, Mark Webster, and Fabian O. Olaz

Experiencing Compassion-Focused Therapy from the Inside Out: A Self-Practice/Self-Reflection Workbook for Therapists by Russell L. Kolts, Tobyn Bell, James Bennett-Levy, and Chris Irons

The Heart of ACT: Developing a Flexible, Process-Based, and Client-Centered Practice Using Acceptance and Commitment Therapy by Robyn D. Walser

Mindfulness for Two: An Acceptance and Commitment Therapy Approach to Mindfulness in Psychotherapy by Kelly G. Wilson and Troy DuFrene

Values in Therapy: A Clinician's Guide to Helping Clients Explore Values, Increase Psychological Flexibility, and Live a More Meaningful Life by Jenna LeJeune and Jason B. Luoma

Acknowledgments

We would like to thank New Harbinger Publications, especially our editors Elizabeth Hollis Hansen, Vicraj Gill, and James Lainsbury, for helping to shape and refine the manuscript, and Matthew McKay for getting us started. Thank you to Easan Drury and Craig Schneider, for feedback and help with the manuscript, and Robyn Walser for writing the foreword.

Our podcast, *Psychologists Off the Clock,* provided the inspiration and spirit behind this book. Thank you to our current and past cohosts (Yael Schonbrun, Jill Stoddard, and Rae Littlewood), interns (Katharine Foley-Saldeña, Kati Lear, Katy Rothfelder, and Melissa Miller), technical producer (Craig Schneider), content strategist (Michael Herold), guests, and listeners. What an enriching experience the podcast has been. We've learned so much from all of you!

The Association for Contextual Behavioral Science, the professional organization for ACT, has been a source of community and intellectual richness beyond any we've experienced. And to the cofounders of ACT, and to all who have contributed to contextual behavioral science over the years, thank you.

Thank you to the other three members of "El Five"—Meg McKelvie, Alexis Kerris Bachik, and Rae Littlewood. You brought us together, and you've inspired us. We love you.

Diana: Thank you to my parents, Helena and Gary, and my sister, Ashley. Mom, you are a true mother hen. Thank you for hatching me, and for now helping hatch my boys with such care. Dad, you are the best storyteller I know. Thank you for your compassion, support, and spiritual wisdom. To my clients, the moments we've shared mean more to me than you know. You've taught me about bravery and what it means to be human. And to my supervisees over the years, I learned so much about ACT by doing it with you. Special thanks to Katharine Foley-Saldeña for your tireless work, flexibility, and shared understanding of working motherhood, and to Michelle

Keane for your methodical and kind guidance. In deep gratitude for my academic and spiritual teachers who have guided me and reminded me to keep on painting, imperfections and all. Special thanks to Linda Craighead, Debra Safer, Alisha Brosse, Malia Sperry, Steven Hayes, Kelly Wilson, Rick Hanson, Anne van de Water, Francie White, and, my first spiritual teacher, Thich Nhat Hanh. Thank you to the training institutions UC Santa Barbara, CU Boulder department of psychology and neuroscience, La Luna Center, and UC Davis CAPS. A big hug and thank you to my dear friends for loving me as I am. Debbie, for taking on this project with me—working with you has been wonderful. To my sons, Henry and Walker, thank you for forcing me to be more flexible, making me laugh, and opening my heart in ways I never imagined. And to Craig, my master beekeeper, you live out your values in all you do and keep our little hive buzzing along. I love you.

Debbie: I would like to thank my supportive network of parents, siblings, friends, neighbors, and extended family members. I am so fortunate to have each and every one of you in my life! Thank you, Diana, for the opportunity to collaborate on this book and the podcast, and for your creativity, openness, and support. Couldn't have done it without you! Thank you to my professional colleagues and clients, past and present, who have been my formal and informal teachers: the Rocky Mountain Regional VA Medical Center (including my colleagues, trainees over the years, and veterans), the national VA ACT for depression training program, the Women in ACBS Special Interest Group, my graduate school and clinical training cohorts, ImpACT Psychology Colorado, and my Colorado private practice therapist friends. I have been inspired by each and every one of you, and you are the reason I love my work! Special thanks to Sean Barnes, Lauren Borges, Kevan McCutcheon, Miranda Morris, and Robyn Walser, for encouraging my passion for ACT and for opening doors for me. I am grateful to have all of you as my colleagues and friends. Thank you to my daughters, Hadley and Piper, for entertaining yourselves while I wrote, and for being wonderful human beings. I love you to pieces. Easan, thank you for the extra kid duty, writing feedback, and, most of all, for being an amazing partner through life's ups and downs.

References

Allione, T. 2008. *Feeding Your Demons: Ancient Wisdom for Resolving Inner Conflict.* Boston: Little, Brown and Company.

Atkins, P.W.B., D.S. Wilson, and S.C. Hayes. 2019. *Prosocial: Using Evolutionary Science to Build Productive, Equitable, and Collaborative Groups.* Oakland, CA: Context Press.

Biglan, A. 2015. *The Nurture Effect: How the Science of Human Behavior Can Improve Our Lives and Our World.* Oakland, CA: New Harbinger Publications.

Bowman, K. 2017. *Move Your DNA: Restore Your Health Through Natural Movement.* 2nd ed. Carlsborg, WA: Propriometrics Press.

Buettner, D. 2008. *The Blue Zones: 9 Lessons for Living Longer from the People Who've Lived the Longest.*

Washington, DC: National Geographic Society.

Chawla, N., and B. Ostafin. 2007. "Experiential Avoidance as a Functional Dimensional Approach to Psychopathology: An Empirical Review." *Journal of Clinical Psychology* 63 (9): 871–90.

Chödrön, P. 2001. *The Wisdom of No Escape and the Path of Loving-Kindness.* Boulder, CO: Shambhala Publications.

Craighead, L.W. 2006. *The Appetite Awareness Workbook: How to Listen to Your Body and Overcome Bingeing, Overeating, and Obsession with Food.* Oakland, CA: New Harbinger Publications.

Dalai Lama, D. Tutu, and D.C. Abrahams. 2016. *The Book of Joy: Lasting Happiness in a Changing World.* New York: Avery.

Diener, E., and M.E.P. Seligman. 2002. "Very Happy People." *Psychological Science* 13 (1): 81–84.

Dweck, C.S. 2016. *Mindset: The New Psychology of Success.* New York: Ballantine Books.

Eyal, N. 2019. *Indistractable: How to Control Your Attention and Choose Your Life.* Dallas: BenBella Books.

Fogg, B.J. 2019. *Tiny Habits: The Small Changes That Change Everything.* Boston: Houghton Mifflin Harcourt.

Forsyth, J.P., and T.R. Ritzert. 2018. "Cultivating Psychological Acceptance." In *Process-Based CBT: The Science and Core Clinical Competencies of Cognitive Behavioral Therapy,* edited by S.C. Hayes and S.G. Hofmann, 363–74. Oakland, CA: Context Press.

Franklin, M.S., M.D. Mrazek, C.L. Anderson, J. Smallwood, A. Kingstone, and J.W. Schooler. 2013. "The Silver Lining of a Mind in the Clouds: Interesting Musings Are Associated with

Positive Mood While Mind-Wandering." *Frontiers in Psychology* 4: 583.

Gilbert, P. 2014. "The Origins and Nature of Compassion Focused Therapy." *British Journal of Clinical Psychology* 53 (1): 6–14.

Gilbert, P. 2017. *Living Like Crazy*. New York: Annwyn House.

Gilbert, P., and Choden. 2014. *Mindful Compassion: How the Science of Compassion Can Help You Understand Your Emotions, Live in the Present, and Connect Deeply with Others*. Oakland, CA: New Harbinger Publications.

Gobin, R.L. 2019. "The Self-Care Prescription with Dr. Robyn Gobin." *Psychologists Off the Clock* (podcast), episode 105, September 21, produced by D. Hill. https://www.offtheclockpsych.com/podcast/self-care-prescription.

Goleman, D. 2005. *Emotional Intelligence: Why It Can Matter More Than IQ*. New York: Bantam Books.

Goleman, D., and R.J. Davidson. 2017. *Altered Traits: Science Reveals How Meditation Changes Your Mind, Brain, and Body.* New York: Avery.

Gottman, J., and N. Silver. 2013. *What Makes Love Last? How to Build Trust and Avoid Betrayal.* New York: Simon & Schuster.

Greaney, M.L., E. Puleo, K. Sprunck-Harrild, J. Haines, S.C. Houghton, and K.M. Emmons. 2018. "Social Support for Changing Multiple Behaviors: Factors Associated with Seeking Support and the Impact of Offered Support." *Health Education and Behavior* 45 (2): 198–206.

Hanson, R. 2018. *Resilient: How to Grow an Unshakable Core of Calm, Strength, and Happiness.* New York: Penguin Random House.

Hanson, R. 2020a. *Neurodharma: New Science, Ancient Wisdom, and Seven Practices of the Highest Happiness.* New York: Harmony Books.

Hanson, R. 2020b. "Taking in the Good with Dr. Rick Hanson." *Psychologists Off the Clock* (podcast), episode 122, January 15, produced by D. Hill. https://www.offtheclockpsych.com/podcast/developing-resilience.

Harris, R. 2019. *ACT Made Simple: An Easy-to-Read Primer on Acceptance and Commitment Therapy.* Oakland, CA: New Harbinger Publications.

Hayes, S.C. 2019. *A Liberated Mind: How to Pivot Toward What Matters.* New York: Avery.

Hayes, S.C., K.D. Strosahl, and K.G. Wilson. 2012. *Acceptance and Commitment Therapy: The Process and Practice of Mindful Change.* 2nd ed. New York: Guilford Press.

Hill, D. 2019a. "A Gift for You: 10 Minute Breathing Meditation." *Psychologists Off the Clock* (podcast), episode 81, March 13, produced by D. Hill. https://www.offtheclockpsych.com/podcast/breathing-meditation.

Hill, D. 2019b. "A Gift for You: Soothing Rhythm Breathing." *Psychologists Off the Clock* (podcast), episode 89, May 9, produced by D. Hill. https://www.oftheclockpsych.com/podcast/soothing-rhythm-breathing.

Holt-Lunstad, J., T.F. Robles, and D.A. Sbarra. 2017. "Advancing Social Connection as a Public Health Priority in the United States." *American Psychologist* 72 (6): 517–30.

hooks, b. 2001. *All About Love: New Visions.* New York: First Perennial.

Huta, V., and R.M. Ryan. 2010. "Pursuing Pleasure or Virtue: The Differential and Overlapping Well-Being Benefits of Hedonic and Eudaimonic Motives." *Journal of Happiness Studies* 11: 735–62.

Kabat-Zinn, J., L. Lipworth, and R. Burney. 1985. "The Clinical Use of Mindfulness Meditation for the Self-Regulation of Chronic Pain." *Journal of Behavioral Medicine* 8 (2):163–90.

Kabat-Zinn, J., A.O. Massion, J. Kristeller, L.G. Peterson, K.E. Fletcher, L. Pbert, W.R. Lenderking, and S.F. Santorelli. 1992. "Effectiveness of a Meditation-Based Stress Reduction Program in the Treatment of Anxiety Disorders." *American Journal of Psychiatry* 149 (7): 936–43.

Killingsworth, M.A., and D.T. Gilbert. 2010. "A Wandering Mind Is an Unhappy Mind." *Science* 330 (6006): 932.

Kolts, R. 2016. *CFT Made Simple: A Clinician's Guide to Practicing Compassion-Focused Therapy.* Oakland, CA: New Harbinger Publications.

Kolts, R. 2018. "Compassion Focused Therapy with Dr. Russell Kolts." *Psychologists Off the Clock* (podcast), episode 50, July 3, produced by *Psychologists Off the Clock.* https://www.offtheclockpsych.com/podcast/compassion-focused-therapy.

LeJeune, J. 2019. "Building a Meaningful, Values-Based Life with Dr.

Jenna LeJeune." *Psychologists Off the Clock* (podcast), episode 116, December 4, produced by D. Sorensen. https://www.offtheclockpsych.com/podcast/values-in-therapy.

Lynch, T.R. 2018. *Radically Open Dialectical Behavior Therapy: Theory and Practice for Treating Disorders of Overcontrol.* Oakland, CA: Context Press.

McGonigal, K. 2019. *The Joy of Movement: How Exercise Helps Us Find Happiness, Hope, Connection, and Courage.* New York: Avery.

McHugh L., I. Stewart, and P. Almada. 2019. *A Contextual Behavioral Guide to the Self: Theory and Practice.* Oakland, CA: Context Press.

McKay, M., and A. West. 2016. *Emotion Efficacy Therapy: A Brief, Exposure-Based Treatment for Emotion Regulation Integrating ACT and DBT.* Oakland, CA: Context Press.

McKay, M., J. Wood, and J. Brantley. 2019. *The Dialectical Behavior Therapy Skills Workbook: Practical DBT Exercises for Learning Mindfulness, Interpersonal Effectiveness, Emotion Regulation, and Distress Tolerance.* Oakland, CA: New Harbinger Publications.

Merwin, R. 2020. "ACT for Food Restriction and Anorexia with Dr. Rhonda Merwin." *Psychologists Off the Clock* (podcast), episode 128, February 26, produced by D. Hill. https://www.offtheclockpsych.com/podcast/act-for-anorexia.

Merwin, R.M., N.L. Zucker, and K.G. Wilson. 2019. *ACT for Anorexia Nervosa: A Guide for Clinicians.* New York: Guilford Press.

Miller, W.R., and S. Rollnick. 2012. *Motivational Interviewing: Helping People Change.* 3rd ed. New York: Guilford Press.

Mohr, T. 2014. *Playing Big: Practical Wisdom for Women Who Want to*

Speak Up, Create, and Lead. New York: Avery.

Moran, D.J., P.A. Bach, and S.V. Batten. 2018. *Committed Action in Practice: A Clinician's Guide to Assessing, Planning, and Supporting Change in Your Client.* Oakland, CA: Context Press.

Neff, K. 2015. *Self-Compassion: The Proven Power of Being Kind to Yourself.* New York: William Morrow.

Neville, H. 2020. "The Psychology of Radical Healing Collective." *Psychologists Off the Clock* (podcast), episode 156, August 6, produced by D. Hill. https://www.offtheclockpsych.com/podcast/the-psychology-of-radical-healing-collective.

Nhat Hanh, Thich 2003. *No Death, No Fear: Comforting Wisdom for Life.* New York: Riverhead Books.

Polk, K.L., B. Shoendorff, M. Webster, and F.O. Olaz. 2016. *The Essential Guide to the ACT Matrix: A Step-by-Step Approach to Using the*

ACT Matrix Model in Clinical Practice. Oakland, CA: Context Press.

Porges, S.W. 2011. *The Polyvagal Theory: Neurophysiological Foundations of Emotions, Attachment, Communication, and Self-Regulation.* New York: W.W. Norton.

Preiss, D.D., D. Cosmelli, V. Grau, and D. Ortiz. 2016. "Examining the Influence of Mind Wandering and Metacognition on Creativity in University and Vocational Students." *Learning and Individual Differences* 51: 417–26.

Robinson, P.J., D.A. Gould, and K.D. Strosahl. 2011. *Real Behavior Change in Primary Care: Improving Patient Outcomes and Increasing Job Satisfaction.* Oakland, CA: New Harbinger Publications.

Schonbrun, Y.C. 2014. "A Mother's Ambitions." *New York Times,* July 30. Accessed July 28, 2020. https://opinionator.blogs.nytimes.com/2014/07/30/a-mothers-ambitions.

Schonbrun, Y.C., and E. Corey. 2020. "Work-Life Conflict Can't Be Solved—and That's a Good Thing." *Wall Street Journal,* June 20. Accessed October 19, 2020. https://www.wsj.com/articles/work-life-conflict-cant-be-solvedand-thats-a-good-thing-11593230460.

Smith, E.E. 2017. *The Power of Meaning: Finding Fulfillment in a World Obsessed with Happiness.* New York: Broadway Books.

Stoddard, J.A. 2019. *Be Mighty: A Woman's Guide to Liberation from Anxiety, Worry, and Stress Using Mindfulness and Acceptance.* Oakland, CA: New Harbinger Publications.

Teasdale, J.D., Z.V. Segal, J.M. Williams, V.A. Ridgeway, J.M. Soulsby, and M.A. Lau. 2000. "Prevention of Relapse/Recurrence in Major Depression by Mindfulness-Based Cognitive Therapy." *Journal of Consulting and Clinical Psychology* 68 (4): 615–23.

Tedeschi, R.G., and L.G. Calhoun. 2004. "Posttraumatic Growth: Conceptual Foundations and Empirical Evidence." *Psychological Inquiry* 15 (1): 1–18.

Tomasello, M. 2014. "The Ultra-Social Animal." *European Journal of Social Psychology* 44 (3): 187–94.

Vanderkam, L. 2018. *Off the Clock: Feel Less Busy While Getting More Done.* New York: Portfolio/Penguin.

Villatte, M., J.L. Villatte, and S.C. Hayes, 2016. *Mastering the Clinical Conversation: Language as Intervention.* New York: Guilford Press.

Walser, R.D. 2019. *The Heart of ACT: Developing a Flexible, Process-Based, and Client-Centered Practice Using Acceptance and Commitment Therapy.* Oakland, CA: Context Press.

Wegner, D.M., D.J. Schneider, S.R. Carter III, and T.L. White. 1987. "Paradoxical Effects of Thought Suppression." *Journal of Personality and Social Psychology* 53 (1): 5–13.

Wilson, K.G., and T. DuFrene. 2009. *Mindfulness for Two: An Acceptance and Commitment Therapy Approach to Mindfulness in Psychotherapy.* Oakland, CA: New Harbinger Publications.

Witkiewitz, K., S. Bowen, H. Douglas, and S.H. Hsu. 2013. "Mindfulness-Based Relapse Prevention for Substance Craving." *Addictive Behaviors* 38 (2): 1563–71.

Yang, L. 2017. *Awakening Together: The Spiritual Practice of Inclusivity and Community.* Boston: Wisdom Publications.

Diana Hill, PhD, is a clinical psychologist in private practice in Santa Barbara, CA, where she provides therapy, high-performance coaching, and training to mental health professionals in acceptance and commitment therapy (ACT). She is cohost of the *Psychologists Off the Clock* podcast, and is passionate about integrative health, homesteading, and parenting with intention.

Debbie Sorensen, PhD, is a clinical psychologist in private practice in Denver, CO, and part-time clinical research psychologist at the Rocky Mountain Regional VA Medical Center. She received her PhD in psychology from Harvard University. Sorensen cohosts the *Psychologists Off the Clock* podcast, and is a VA regional trainer and training consultant in acceptance and commitment therapy (ACT).

MORE BOOKS *from* NEW HARBINGER PUBLICATIONS

A MOMENT FOR ME
52 Simple Mindfulness Practices to Slow Down, Relieve Stress, and Nourish the Spirit

REVEAL PRESS
An Imprint of New Harbinger Publications

ANXIETY HAPPENS
52 Ways to Find Peace of Mind

THE MIND-BODY STRESS RESET
Somatic Practices to Reduce Overwhelm and Increase Well-Being

THE INTUITIVE EATING WORKBOOK
Ten Principles for Nourishing a Healthy Relationship with Food

THE UNTETHERED SOUL
The Journey Beyond Yourself

MINDFULNESS FOR INSOMNIA
A Four-Week Guided Program to Relax Your Body, Calm Your Mind, and Get the Sleep You Need

newharbingerpublications
1-800-748-6273 / newharbinger.com
(VISA, MC, AMEX / prices subject to change without notice)   Follow Us

Don't miss out on new books in the subjects that interest you.
Sign up for our Book Alerts at **newharbinger.com/bookalerts**

Register your **new harbinger** titles for additional benefits!

When you register your **new harbinger** title—purchased in any format, from any source—you get access to benefits like the following:

- Downloadable accessories like printable worksheets and extra content
- Instructional videos and audio files
- Information about updates, corrections, and new editions

Not every title has accessories, but we're adding new material all the time.

Access free accessories in 3 easy steps:

1. Sign in at NewHarbinger.com (or **register** to create an account).

2. Click on **register a book**. Search for your title and click the **register** button when it appears.

3. Click on the **book cover or title** to go to its details page. Click on **accessories** to view and access files.

That's all there is to it!

If you need help, visit:

NewHarbinger.com/accessories

Back Cover Material

"Both simple and profound, practical and soulful, healing and inspiring.... A real gem."
—Rick Hanson, PhD, author of *Hardwiring Happiness*

"I highly recommend ACT Daily Journal."
—Steven C. Hayes, PhD, originator of ACT and author of *A Liberated Mind*

Let This Journal Guide You Toward What Really Matters

In our hectic and increasingly uncertain world, it's easy to lose track of what's important and get bogged down by daily stress. We all want to savor the deeper, more meaningful experiences of life, but many of us feel too stuck, distracted, anxious, and overwhelmed to live fully in the moment. If you're looking for ways to slow down and reconnect with what *really* matters to you, this journal can help spark the positive change you crave.

With *ACT Daily Journal,* you'll find powerful writing practices grounded in acceptance and commitment therapy (ACT) to help you get unstuck and start loving your life. You'll learn how to stay present in the moment, focus on your values, balance your emotions, and gain the mental flexibility you need to thrive in difficult situations. If there were ever a time to commit to living according to what you *truly* care about, it's now. So, what are you waiting for?

www.ingramcontent.com/pod-product-compliance
Lightning Source LLC
Chambersburg PA
CBHW011959150426
43201CB00019B/2330